Invisible Ink

Carl A. Veno

PublishAmerica
Baltimore

First printing

Cover Photo credits:
Headshot is by Church Impressions, Inc.

ISBN: 1-4137-4881-3
PUBLISHED BY PUBLISHAMERICA, LLLP
www.publishamerica.com
Baltimore

Printed in the United States of America

To Luigi and Anna Veno, my parents,
the smartest people I ever knew.

Acknowledgments

No book has ever been written without the help of many minds. I am grateful for those who contributed editorial support to *Invisible Ink*. I have interviewed hundreds of people; some would talk, and others would not. I tried to contact many. Some would not even take my calls.

I am totally indebted to Sue Long Turner, who is an editing genius. The author of *Wings Born Out of Dust,* Sue shaped the creativity that *Invisible Ink* needed. I thank the NASA History Web Curator, Steve Garber, Jack Snyder of the *Orlando Sentinel,* Nat Bodian of the *Newark News,* the website of the *Late Great Pennsylvania Station,* Harry McGavish, founder of the Park Bench Gang, William Fote, researchers Donna Smith, Anne Baldwin, Anthony Veno, Carla Jones, Iz Barmash of the *New York Times,* Joe and Rita Veno, *Tiger at the Bar* by Chester Harris, the Baumgratz Publishing company of Ridgway, Pennsylvania, Bucks County Travel Net, Lehigh County Court records, the *Orlando Sentinel,* the Quakertown Library, the *Hudson Dispatch,* the *Bergen Record,* the *Newark News,* the *Quakertown Free Press,* the *Yonkers Herald Statesman,* the *Mount Vernon Argus,* the Newark, New Jersey Public Library archives, Professor Stephen Fox, author of *The Unknown Internment of Italian Americans,* designer Miguel Rivera, the Yonkers Public Library, and my wife, Attorney Linda Luther-Veno.

Because of the sensitive nature of some of the stories, some names have been changed for obvious reasons. When a pseudonym is used, the name appears for the first time with an asterisk, as in "Sam A. Smith*."

Contents

Introduction

First you destroy those who create values. Then you destroy those who know what the values are.
—Ryzard Kapuscinski, Polish Journalist

Fortunately for America, Charles Meredith III, my final newspaper boss, published the *Free Press* in Bucks County, Pennsylvania, and not the *Washington Post*. Imagine this scenario: Meredith publishes the *Post* at the time of Watergate. He fires Reporters Bob Woodward and Carl Bernstein. For good measure, mentally and emotionally blind, Charles tosses *Washington Post* Editor Ben Bradley in the discard bin. President Richard Nixon completes his term as President.

The United States would have avoided the biggest scandal in American history. Most abhorrent of all, we would have failed to test that clause in the Constitution that proves the President of the United States is not above the law.

Unlike the gutsy *Washington Post* Publisher, Katherine Graham, Meredith panicked at the words *sources, said, it has been reported, or questioned.* He had no inkling that newspapers need these tools to protect unidentified sources and move government agencies to reveal information.

Investigative reporting terrified Meredith. "Elected officials shouldn't be held to the highest standards in the land," he said. "Newspapers aren't watchdogs over our government."

He couldn't understand that if politicians blink in the wrong direction, the press has not only an obligation, but also a responsibility to report it. Charles Meredith III would rather sink the potential powerhouse story than question the actions of a politician. Being a politician himself made him leery of the press, the very institution that for three generations made the Merediths wealthy. In his viewpoint, those news stories were written to wrap around ads.

According to Kapuscinski, the Polish Journalist, real barbarism begins when no one can any longer judge or know that what he does is barbaric. There you have a picture-perfect likeness of Charles Meredith III.

I can only be humble and grateful that from my roots out of dry ground sprang a journalist with an eye toward creating and upholding values.

Chapter 1
West 46th Street

All glory comes from daring to begin.
—Anonymous

"One room and a communal bathroom, and that ain't bad for fourteen dollars a week. Yeah, right in the middle of Manhattan."

The desk clerk brushed the cigarette ashes from his trousers and straightened his wrinkled red tie. With his handkerchief he wiped his sweaty forehead, some food crumbs from around his mouth, and finished his sales pitch.

The gray stucco apartment building on West 46th in New York City looked more inviting on the outside than the inside. The lobby's wallpaper, peeling and turning brown, had faded to a dingy white. The place was stuffy and hot.

So this is a flophouse?

What a dump. The musty smell sickened me.

"What's that terrible odor?" I asked.

"We got to sanitize the place."

No doubt roaches and ants crawled around the rooms. Probably loaded with rats, too. I hated this place, but the rent was affordable.

"I'll take it."

"How long you planning on staying?"

"A few months, if I can survive the roaches."

He muttered without looking up, "You will."

After arriving in the Big Apple on a hot, oppressive July afternoon in 1958, I wanted nothing more than to cool off, settle down, and get some chow. It had been a long 400 miles.

Every bone in my body ached. The eight-hour bumpy bus ride from Olean, New York, wore me down. I was exhausted.

Waiting for room keys, I returned to thoughts of early morning and the farewell send-off from a few of the Park Bench Gang at the bus depot.

The guys were certain I had lost my mind when I announced my plans to head for New York City to make a fortune as a professional prizefighter.

"On your way, stop at the nuthouse and have them check you out," one of the guys yelled as the bus pulled away.

The odds of making it big in New York City at any endeavor is astronomical, but so what? The chances are still better here in New York City then the small town I just left.

Talent, timing, and luck, so I'm told, hit a home run for a successful life. If one is missing, you strike out. I was about to find out if I had two "Ts" and an "L."

Of all the difficult jobs I had to try, prizefighting proved the toughest and bloodiest. You never find a way around getting your brains rattled.

Finally, dangling the key inches from my nose, the clerk, with tiny, silver bifocals resting on his nose, warned me what lies ahead if you don't pay the rent.

"And remember," he said, looking straight into my eyes, "the rent is always paid in advance on Monday. If not, see that sidewalk outside the lobby door? That's where you'll land. On your ass. The name Pete Moss won't even be on the eviction papers. We don't want to hear any bullshit stories. We have heard them all. On time."

I reached down, got a firm grip on my only suitcase, and with the other hand wiped the dripping sweat off my forehead.

"I understand." I started to walk away, but the clerk continued his monologue.

"I know it's none of my business, kid, but what the hell are you doing in New York City?"

I told him I fought as a professional prizefighter and I'd be working out at Stillman's Gym on Eighth Avenue, a few blocks away.

He continued to stare, eyeing me up and down, bifocals intensifying his hard look.

His hand moved to adjust the eyeglasses. "You look like fresh meat. All the fighters I see around here end up with banana noses, scarred faces, and are brain dead from the looks of 'em."

"Not me. When I get to the top, I'm leaving with all my marbles."

His smile changed to a smirk.

"Get to the top first, kid."

I had not heard it all yet from the clerk.

"There aren't too many real men in this building. Let me give you some fatherly advice, kid. Watch out for the fags. They're all over."

I gazed at him, a little puzzled. "Why should I be worried?"

"You'll see."

I assured him I could take care of myself and headed for the elevators that took me to the 14th floor.

I got off the elevator and I caught the nauseous pesticide stink again. There must have been roaches all over this place. Exposed food in the tenants' rooms undoubtedly whetted the roaches' appetites.

I wouldn't live here long.

I walked toward the end of the tiny hallway and saw the communal bathroom that I'd share with ten other male tenants.

Wow, I couldn't believe my eyes. The condition of the three rusty sinks and three shower stalls made my stomach turn. The tile walls were brownish yellow, worn thin, and undistinguishable. A real shithouse.

My room consisted of a cot, a dresser, and a window with no air conditioning.

It resembled a large closet. With the heat so oppressive, I rushed to the window and yanked it open. No help. The outside Manhattan afternoon breeze added to the scorching heat inside. The nights would cool things off.

I unpacked my suitcase, grabbed a change of clothes, and headed

13

for Stillman's to meet my future manager, Frankie Madden. I walked along Eighth Avenue and thought about the beginnings of this New York journey.

A lifetime friend, Joe Pezzamenti, a pizza restaurant owner, a hustler, was now a fight manager. Joe contacted Madden. He worked for the now defunct *Herald Journal American* newspaper and according to Joe, he had good sports connections. Joe assured me that Madden would also provide me with great trainers.

When I worked out in Olean, Joe would let me use the back room of his pizzeria to train. Joe had a little bed there and every day while I pounded on a heavy sandbag, he took a nap and always had the same dream about getting rich without working. Joe was the talk of the town, and he didn't exactly come out on the plus side. He never managed to veer from the gossip mill.

I guess there is a Joe in every town. Are they misfits or do we need them around to boost our own self-esteem? Listen to the local gossip at the coffee shops and the people like Joe will be the major topic.

In spite of his faults, I liked Joe. He spoke truthfully to me, and that's all I expected. Pezzy, as everyone called him, was a small-built man with narrow waist, big nose, large brown eyes, and no hair on his head. He resembled Jimmy Durante.

At first I was reluctant to go to New York City.

I explained to Joe that I had little experience at boxing and it was possible that I could lose a few of my marbles with the top fighters.

"Don't worry. You're a tough kid, and you'll be able to handle yourself with little trouble," he said. " And with Frankie helping you're bound to do well ..."

His support helped, but I had already made up my mind. I thought, what the hell? If it gets too rough I can always quit; besides, my opportunities in Olean were less than zero.

Just before three o'clock, I walked at a good pace along the busy sidewalk toward the gym. I felt good and was almost unaware of the heat and the horns honking and sirens wailing.

"Hey, I'm in New York City, a place where dreams come true, "I spoke aloud to the City, its people, its buildings.

When I arrived at Stillman's Gym entrance, I saw an arrow pointing to the second floor. On the first floor there was a candy store that tempted even the most dedicated health nuts. I'd learn that the place had terrific ice cream malts. At the top of the stairs, before I could go into the gym, a rugged ex-fighter blocked my entrance. He sat on a high chair with one of his legs stretched across the door.

"There's a price to get in here kid—two dollars to you." he said.

"I have an appointment to see Frankie Madden."

"Wait here."

I could hear the rhythm of the punching bags from inside the gym and the big thuds of the fighters hitting the big sandbags. The odor was that thick, stinging smell that hovers over busy gyms. The gatekeeper returned with a short, heavyset man. He wore his black hair slicked back and covering his ears. He wore a double-breasted blue suit and chewed on an unlighted cigar.

"Carl?"

"You, of course, are Mr. Madden."

He smiled, waved me in, and escorted me to a few metal chairs surrounding the two boxing rings.

I was finally inside the famous Stillman's Gym, a place where all the great champions come to train.

"I talked to Joe, and here is what I want you to do," Frankie said. "Do you have a place to stay?"

I lowered my head and muttered the name.

"I know it's a dump, but wait about a month, and we will find something better."

He talked on and on about the training schedule. I nodded my head with approval.

"I'll drop in weekly to check on you. Dan Florio and Izzy Kline will help. Don't expect too much from them. They are busy guys."

Wow! Famous trainers—I'd read about them in *Ring Magazine*. They were known to handle top-rated fighters. As a favor to Madden they would give me some of their time. I was thrilled.

"Before you leave, I want to get you a membership and introduce you to Lou Stillman, the owner of the gym."

We both walked over to Stillman. He held a microphone to introduce each fighter sparring in the two large boxing rings in front of him. Frank told me Stillman turned the ceremony into a tradition that he cherished.

So this was Lou Stillman.

He was a thin man in his fifties, with a long nose, sparse white hair, and blue eyes. He stood a little under six feet as he strode about his gym. Not a friendly guy; he seemed uncomfortable around me. After meeting me, he gave me a quick handshake and walked away.

I heard he could be a mean son of a bitch. I never expected to talk to him again. However, I didn't lose any sleep over the cool relationship. When he had to announce my name as a sparring partner, it was obvious that to say it just about killed him. One of the fighters told me that he always carried a gun. I never wanted to find out.

Frankie went over the final instructions before he left.

"Get to the gym every day at noon, train hard, we'll get you a fight in about three weeks," he said. "I'll get you lined up with a four-rounder on the boxing card at Fort Hamilton in Brooklyn."

Whew! Could I be ready that fast?

"Fast plans are on because you must pay your own way. No free lunches here." He reminded me that anything he paid for would have to be paid back off the top of the proceeds.

"There's a restaurant about a block down from here. It's called the Neutral Corner." Frankie gestured in the direction of the restaurant. "It's a bar and with a lunch counter. You can meet a lot of fighters there." Madden put the cigar back in the corner of his mouth each time he paused to take a breath. "Tony Genaro is the bartender, tough fighter from Youngstown, Ohio, once a top contender. Tell him you're working for me. He'll take care of you."

I shook his hand.

"Frankie, I will do my best for you."

"I know you will, kid." He shook my hand again, and then he hurried down the gym stairs and disappeared into the crowded street.

I decided to walk over to the Neutral Corner and see if I could meet some of the fighters. When I walked in, I saw a bunch of guys at the lunch counter. Without missing a step, I straightened my shoulders and introduced myself to the one closest to me. Rich English was an ex-hockey player from Toronto. Although he had ten fights in Canada, his face was loaded with scar tissue from the hockey fights he'd encountered over the years.

He shook my hand with an iron grip.

"We all want to make a killing without getting killed," was his favorite saying, I found out when we became good friends. I saw him in the gym during the day and hung around with him nights.

Rich introduced me to some of the other young boxers, and one fighter struck me as extremely young—I mean, he looked like a child.

"Hi, Carl," he said with a big smile. "I'm Fred Piper from Rochester. My father owns a gym there and he sent me here to train, get a few fights, and make a name for myself."

He looked like someone who should be in grammar school, not a fighter. He had black hair, a baby face, and weighed about 145. When I found out his age—15, I thought to myself that this guy was going to get killed.

Boy was I wrong. He was a great boxer and dancer who had the speed of a famous featherweight, Willie Pep. Although I did not pal with Fred, we became friends while I was staying in New York. He lived about a block away.

After gulping down a soda and a roast beef sandwich, I said goodbye to the guys and hurried back to my apartment. After I had unpacked, something else I wanted to do sent me flying to the streets.

This wasn't my first trip to New York, so I knew my way around. I decided to walk over to Central Park and map out the path where I would be doing my roadwork. Still exhausted from the long day, I sat on a park bench next to a sleeping homeless guy. It was such a sad sight to see these poor souls living their strange lives. Many were alcoholics, ex-mental patients, and drug addicts. I was always charitable to the unfortunates. I was born a soft touch. As soon as he knew there was someone next to him, he jumped out and began begging for money. I did not preach to him or say a word. I just reached in my pocket gave him a five-dollar bill. I knew it was not the right thing to do, but what the hell. His eyes brightened up and he looked like he just hit the lottery.

"Thanks," he said. "I'll get some food with this."

The last thing he would do was eat. "Yeah, right!" He didn't hear, though. That guy was long gone to the nearest liquor store.

After a few hours of walking around Central Park, I headed back to the apartment for a nap, heat or no heat. It was still too hot to rest. So I got dressed, went down to the lobby, walked outside, and I sat on the stoop. A few minutes later up came Fred, the young kid I met at noon.

"Hey, Carl, let's get something to eat at the Neutral Corner."

We both walked to the restaurant and sat at the lunch counter. Fred chatted with just about everyone. He apparently was well-known and well-liked.

"What are you going to do for excitement?" he asked.

"Fred, I just got here, and besides I'm going to live a Trappist Monk's life for a while. I need to get in shape and stay out of trouble and get plenty of sleep."

"You got to have some fun or you won't function." He gave me that big smile. "Listen, I know where there are a lot of girls craving to go out and it's only a few blocks from here. They come in by the droves every day—from would-be models to runaways. They're all looking for a good time. You don't have to be serious with them or spend any money on them. Just screw them and leave them."

"No. Not me."

"And did you know there are a lot of fags out there, and they will pay you for going to bed with them."

I couldn't believe what I heard. This young kid made money as a part-time male prostitute. How sick.

"You got to be nuts," I said. " I would leave those people alone."

"Someone has to take care of them," he said. "I know a Frenchman who wants to take good care me of and he pays me good, too. How do you think I live here? And when the Ice Capades are in town, I make a killing. Did you know a lot of those skaters are fags?"

"When do you find time to fight and train?"

"I don't need much training. I do well without it."

When he obviously could tell I was disgusted, he changed the subject.

"I got to go, I'll see you tomorrow at the gym," I said.

"Carl, I'm young but not dumb. I've learned how to survive out there in the mean world. Get what you can from anyone who gives. Don't be a crusader."

"I'm not a crusader, I'm a fighter."

"You won't make it if you don't have a killer instinct," he said, and we parted company.

Maybe he was right, and then I put that out of my mind. Darkness came on to match my mood, and I was dead tired. Walking up the street, I noticed a number of street hookers who had started on their night's work. I stayed clear of them, never glancing in their direction. If you were alone and a male, they would drive you nuts.

Sleep. That's what I needed, sleep.

I went up to my room, undressed, grabbed my shorts and a towel, and hurried down the hall to take a cold shower. In spite of the conditions of the bathroom, the shower was refreshing.

Out of the shower, I noticed a small elderly gentleman washing his face in the sink next to me. He had a large white towel wrapped around his waist. A bunch of keys dangled from a belt attached to the towel.

"Hi." I added a smile to my greeting

He smiled back. "It's a hot night isn't it?"

"Certainly is."

The shower had cooled me off, but not nearly enough. I had to sleep, since at five a.m. I would be out of bed for my roadwork in Central Park.

I lay down on my cot and decided to keep the door open to create a little breeze in the hot room. I must have fallen asleep before closing the door. A clanging sound opened my eyes. Half asleep, I saw a silhouette of a half-naked person with a towel wrapped around his body. He stood in the open doorway. The hallway light exposed him and I noticed he was the same man I had talked to in the bathroom earlier.

I jumped to my feet. "Get the hell out of here before I throw you out the window."

He started crying. "I'm sorry. I'm terrible sorry. I just can't help myself."

My anger subsided and I said, "You're in the wrong room, sir. I'm sure it was a mistake on your part."

Without a word he hurried down the hall.

What a chance he was taking coming in to my room. Of course, it was no mistake. It was troubling to know that this man would risk getting hurt to satisfy his inner drives. It was just too deep for me to comprehend.

What a day. And what a night. I fell asleep again, this time 'til early morning. I had a fight in three weeks and that's all that was on my mind.

Being a sparring partner had it setbacks. Every fighter used you for a punching bag and you went home every night feeling like you were run over by an army tank. After a while your nose gets as big as a cucumber, and then it breaks and breaks again. Your face hurts even when you get hit with a big glove and wear the proper headgear.

I was always put in with seasoned fighters. It was the only way I could learn fast. I had to spar with Joe Micelli and Patty Young, two real tough guys. When I sparred with these guys, I was way out of my class. Micelli showed a little mercy, but Young was ruthless. He was always trying to knock my head off.

One time he left himself open and I hit with a right hand square on his chin. His knees buckled and I knew I had shaken him up. Before the round ended, we were trading wild punches. He pounded me with scores of hard punches, and I hit with a few good shots, too.

When the round was over, he walked over to me and took his mouthpiece out. "You got a lot of balls, kid, and you hit pretty hard." As friendly as he got, he would never let up on me. Young was a good fighter, but I heard he drank too much.

I saw a lot of good fighters at Stillman's. Hurricane Jackson was one of them. He was a nice guy. I heard he died after a car hit him on a street in New York City.

After weeks of training, I was in shape and ready for my big fight at Fort Hamilton.

At the weigh-in, my opponent, a seasoned professional from the Midwest named Mike Smith, stepped on the scale in front of me. He was taller than I. Dark blond hair and a hawk-like face glared at me. When I saw how much heavier he was than I was, I complained to the doctor and the promoter that he was almost 10 pounds over the then 160-pound limit.

The doctor replied, "Don't worry kid, it's all in his ass."

"He's not going to hit me with his ass, doctor."

Not answering me, he smiled and shouted, "Next fighter."

Rich and Fred were also scheduled to fight at Fort Hamilton, and we were going to get a ride to Brooklyn from Manhattan with Izzy Klein, the trainer.

It was an outdoor arena with the locker rooms under the stands.

We drove to Brooklyn, and Izzy worried about one of his dogs that got sick, but not his fighters. "I hope he is going to be all right," he said. I hoped he worried about us fighters as much as he did about his pet.

"Hope we can wrap this thing up early so I get home and take care of my sweetheart," he said.

We pulled into the parking lot, and I could feel my heart beat a little faster.

I walked toward the locker room, feeling butterflies flip-flop in my stomach. Every fighter gets them. The tension builds and the body stiffens.

I put on my gold boxing trunks, scraped the bottom of my shoes and rested on a chair until someone called my name to go up the wooden stairs to get it on with my opponent. I could hear the screams and yells from the crowd above me. They loved blood and knockouts.

"You're third in line," Kline said. "When you get called, we'll go up the stairs and wait at ringside for the referee to call you in."

As I sat in the chair; the tension heightened. I knew it was going to be a tough fight, but I felt a sense of confidence. I heard he knocked out every one of his ten opponents. Well, he hadn't met me yet.

I stood up to stretch and danced around a little. Suddenly I heard the sound of thunder outside. Oh, no, not rain. Suddenly I heard the clap of thunder and saw flashes of lightning appearing in the little basement windows.

I heard someone running down the stairs. "It's raining like hell. I think they are going to postpone the rest of the fights," the attendant said.

I heard a lot of grumbling.

Just like that, the fight I had been waiting for and training for would be swooped away with the summer rain. All the work down the drain along with my dreams of making it in New York.

Maybe it was not meant to be.

When the raining skies opened that night, maybe it was a message, an intercession, or an act of mercy. Whatever, it worked.

I would box again, but without any enthusiasm. The thrill and excitement left with the storming skies. Whatever happened in Fort Hamilton that night, I got the memo. Time to move on.

Before I left the gym on my final day in New York, Izzy Kline laced the gloves on another young fighter, then he turned to me. "Go back to Buffalo." No matter that I didn't come from Buffalo. "Get more experience and come back—you got a lot of potential. You can really make it in this game."

"Thanks." I walked out of the gym with a lot more confidence than when I arrived, but also with a sense of sadness, and I was too impatient to start from the bottom.

Back at West 46th Street, the desk clerk shuffled papers on his desk and looked up when I came in. "Enjoyed having you here in this homey flophouse," he said as he removed his small eyeglasses. "I heard you got the making of a champion. Do you think you'll ever be back?"

"It's hard to say."

"If you come back in a few years, it will all be gone. New York will, day in and day out, make room for the new, the different. Build it up and tear it down. Nothing is forever."

"I guess you're right. Take care, and thanks for the all fatherly wisdom." I could feel his eyes on me when I walked out the door. I wasn't sure, but I felt it. I'll never know—I didn't turn around to find out.

The bus made its way to the West Side Highway and headed north along the Hudson River toward the George Washington Bridge. I looked across the river at the Palisades, admiring the beauty of it all.

I thought about all the unique friends I'd made in the city. I think of them often and I wonder where they are today. New York City and I hadn't seen the last of each other—not by a long shot.

Down deep in my soul, I knew I would be back. I did not know when, I only knew I would be back.

Twenty years later, I returned to work in New York City as a journalist.

Chapter 2
Buying a Ticket to Paradise

After struggling with mountainside acres of scorched farmland that stubbornly yielded little crop and little hope, my grandfather gave in to his growing yearning to leave Naples, Italy. Carlo Veno, the only child of my great grandparents, at the age of twenty made the decision that would alter the lives of his descendants. It was the late 1800s and thousands of Europeans were leaving abject poverty and crossing the Atlantic to seek a new life in America, the "Promised Land."

"I saved for months to buy a ticket to paradise," my grandfather recalled. "I stuffed what little clothes I owned into a black sheepskin duffel bag, kissed my wife and two children goodbye, and hitched a horse ride to the Naples passenger shipping terminal and said goodbye."

He traveled through Naples, where thirty years earlier the Bourbons controlled the government until it was annexed by the great Italian patriot Garibaldi. Carlo gazed in wide-eyed disbelief at the hawking merchants shouting at the top of their lungs to lure potential customers. Their loud voices flooded the marketplace. From rows of tiny open-air shops, merchants yanked on the sleeves of customers in hopes of enticing a sale. "Buy pure gold jewelry cheap!" Carlo squeezed the money in his front pocket. It was a grip of security. "I can't eat gold."

Carlo caught the smell of fresh roasted garlic. He saw logs of cheese and strings of red peppers dangling in front of the hot grill steaming with meat patties. The delicious odors stirred his appetite and tempted him, but the money he had must be kept for the long journey. Carlo disciplined himself to be an astute steward of his finances. The sporadic sound of the silversmiths shaping dazzling metal ornaments faded into the distance as he left the outskirts of Naples.

Arriving at the departing dock, Carlo witnessed an incredible scene. Swarms of young Italians, as far as his eyes could see, were shoulder to shoulder. Squeezed together, almost glued to each other, they pushed their way near the gangplank, waiting to stampede the German steamer that would take them to the "Promised Land." Maintaining their balance to keep from falling into the water, they were determined not to be left behind. What a sight! "It looked like all the young men, I think, decided to leave Italy at one time," he recalled.

The short, scrappy, muscular Neapolitan had read the encouraging news in a journal that the United States held hope for the downtrodden. Fired up about the opportunities awaiting those who stepped foot on its shores, he wasted little time in moving to the front of the almost riotous crowd.

"If I found a good-paying job and a place to bring my family, then my dream would come true," he said he told a fellow passenger on the ship.

The young, energetic adventure seekers surrounding Carlo yelled and bragged about the big money waiting for them in America. They flexed their muscles, showing what they would use to build their future. Pushing, shoving, and arm wrestling, they matched their strengths with each other. Their hearts and minds were full of hope. Those who could read attempted to decipher the English travel brochures, getting a feel for the foreign geography. Some hung onto their tickets so firmly their hands were blotched with ink. There were those who were so overwhelmed by the chaos they just sat dumfounded on travel bags, shading their olive-skinned faces from the afternoon sun and staring at the blue waters of Naples Bay.

Bored and tired after hours of waiting, the men stretched out, using their travel bags for pillows. Some, still wearing heavy coats, their faces to the blue sky, listened to the honking sounds of distant ships moving in the bay. The almost crushing departure area left little room to walk, forcing the young, mustachioed *paesanos* to hop among their fellow Italians. Boredom did not dull their imaginations as they waited for passage on the German steamer, which eventually set sail for Ellis Island in Upper New York Bay. The long, laborious ten-day voyage consisted of sitting and standing on the decks, sleeping in overcrowded berths, eating a little bread and some sausages, and waiting. The grueling ride and seasickness took some of the wind from the sails of the young men. After long talks about the finding of fortunes, many settled for a resting place on the sweltering, sun-baked deck. The monotonous voyage dulled the minds but not the dreams of these young Romans.

Finally, on the fifth day, a cry came from of the passengers on the port side. "The Statue of Liberty! the Statue of Liberty! We in America!"

"Not quite," my grandfather said. "We have to go to Ellis Island and get our visiting visa."

Ellis Island, the immigration and naturalization center for 12 million Europeans, was flooded with humans as Carlo rushed off the German steamer and toward one of the hundreds of tiny aisles that fed tired immigrants to immigration officials. There the exhausted souls filled out entrance papers, and some who looked ill were separated and given closer physicals.

With their nametags tied to their lapels, they eventually moved from the island to the bustling streets of Manhattan or Newark. Carlo, in New York City, was astounded by what he saw—thousands of horses and carriages and merchants, bars and restaurants, and big signs—"Workers Sign Here" or "Help Wanted, English Language Not Required." The exploitation of cheap help didn't faze the men. They took any job for any money.

"It was a hell of lot more than we made in Italy," he said. Less than twenty-four hours after arriving in paradise, Carlo turned down a railroad job that would have given him a one-way ticket to Kansas City to settle in the Midwest and Indian Territory. "They want bodies in that part of the country for homesteading, any body," said a fellow immigrant.

Instead, Carlo went to work on the Pennsylvania Railroad, living in camp railroad cars, washing his clothes in a small water basin, and eating lunch and dinner while sitting on hot rails.

Like the rest of the European immigrants arriving in the late 1800s, Carlo found the streets of American were not paved with gold, but with dirt, sweat and tough times. The Germans and the Irish who had arrived earlier controlled the good jobs. The Italians were at the bottom of the barrel. Handicapped by a language barrier, Carlo settled for a low-paying, back-breaking, railroad spike-pounding job. Not much of a dream job, he realized. He quit, and reluctantly worked other odds jobs and traveled up to and around the New England states. Disappointed after his visit to America, Carlo decided to go back to the unproductive farmland of Naples to rethink his career.

Back in Naples, he finally realized that America was his future. Carlo did not find his wealth in America, but the handsome Neapolitan did fall in love with traveling. Fascinated by what he saw and what he had learned about the world, Carlo even thought about exploring South America and its treasures. The urge to move gnawed at him. He came back to America, but he would cross the Atlantic four more times before unhappily settling for a job once again as a gandy dancer on the Pennsylvania Railroad in Olean, a small city in Western New York.

Under the blazing-hot summer sun and in the bitter winter cold, Carlo finally earned enough money to bring his family to the United States. One of his sons, Louis, my father, arrived at Ellis Island in 1918. Like his father before him, Louie would not avoid the laborer's sweat. He joined the industrial workforce, picking up a core maker's trade in the Clark Brothers' foundry.

With the help of his wife, Louie's family would truly live the American dream. The family enjoyed a huge home, a pantry loaded with pasta, an overflowing meat freezer, and basement shelves filled with canned tomatoes, beans, corn, peppers, and other delicious vegetables. Louie had a dream vegetable garden, money in the bank, and five healthy, educated children.

Carlo's agonizing decision to stay in America after four trips set the stage and fate of five Veno families and twenty-five Veno children.

As a boy, I remember my grandfather as a white-haired, ruddy-faced, corncob-pipe-smoking, easygoing gentleman. He never talked much, but always appeared to be in deep thought as he walked around his two-bedroom house. A generous man, he always reached in his pocket when he saw his grandchildren coming and would give my brother and sisters and me a nickel. Other times he would give us something out of his vegetable garden.

A self-educated man, Carlo was well read. He loved to listen to Italian music on his oval walnut radio while he sat in his large armchair. The pungent tobacco from his corncob pipe filled the air. I was amazed at this world traveler who would talk to me in broken English about his ventures.

I wish I had been older then to ask him more about his young life. I never knew the reasoning of his four trips. The little time I spent with him made my life richer and gave me a sense of connection to my heritage. Carlo enjoyed great health and died at the age of eighty-nine. After Carlo's death, my grandmother, Jennie, would not live with any of her children. This short, squat, tough woman lived alone in her own house. She planted a garden and raised a goat.

Jennie's browned, weather-beaten face resembled the face of an Indian woman living on the Great Plains. She smiled broadly when she saw a photo of herself in the local newspaper working in her garden at age 92. At one time, she carried the proud title of the oldest Italian woman in Olean.

A doctor never treated Jennie. This hard working gardener never worried and went to bed at seven o'clock every night. She ate greens from her garden, drank goat's milk, and ate little meat. Jennie had the kind of life we all wish for—to live long and healthy and to die in our sleep. We all prayed that we would inherit her genes.

My mother, Anna Veno, was in her teens when she arrived in America from southern Italy with her father and mother. They lived in Zanesville, Ohio, before moving to Dunmore, Pennsylvania. She met my father in Zanesville, and they married in Columbus. My grandfather Philip Veno, a pleasant but high-strung man, worked in the pottery factory in Iron Spot, Ohio, and then in the Pennsylvania coal mines. A hard worker, his eyes were always flashing as if he expected a major catastrophe any second. I remember he came to live with us one summer and he, like my mother, was obsessed with cleaning.

One day a fly got into the house and it upset my grandfather to no end. He spent the better part of a day hunting it down, finally tracking it down under the kitchen window shade and then put an end to the buzzing insect with a swift swing of the fly swatter.

Like my grandmother Jennie, my mother's parents were healthy and lived into their late eighties. They died in Dunmore. I never saw my grandmother on my mother's side, but I did see pictures of her. She was such a woman of beauty. She died in her earlier sixties.

The Veno family settled down and made its mark in Olean, New York. This beautiful western New York community of 16,000 people rests at the foothills of the mighty Allegheny Mountains. It was my home for 29 years. Olean, "The Land of the Enchanted Mountains," is where I spent my inquisitive childhood and my unsettling, active, and dreaming youth.

As a seven-year-old, I would lie in my bed and in late autumn hear the noisy Canada geese flapping their wings as they headed south. Their numbers and sound seemed endless, a melodious reminder that winter winds and snow were not far behind.

The airborne, honking flock played havoc with my imagination, and I longed to be in flight with them.

As a family, we seldom traveled move than fifty miles from home, our biggest thrill being the Clark Brothers' company picnic at Celran Park in Jamestown, New York. The rest of my travels were accomplished by dreams and reading travel magazines.

After school each day, I would take long walks along the stony

Pennsylvania Railroad, tiptoeing on the hot rails. I reached a small path near the railroad that led me to the green forest close to an oil refinery a mile from my house. I climbed the steep hill to the stone quarry landing, my favorite resting spot. Beneath the shade of the giant maples, I cupped my hands and drank the cool, refreshing spring water pouring out of the Rock Mountain. I could look beyond the oil refinery and view the city in the far distance. As it did with my grandfather, an obsession to travel and move from place to place ran through my soul too. The craving for it never left me.

It was the summer of 1944 and World War II was raging in Europe. From my favorite site on the quarry, I watched the heavy rail traffic of military might. I saw miles and miles of troop trains speeding by, blowing their whistles at the crossing, heading for the Philadelphia and New York City waterfronts and then to the war zones. I saw the faces of soldiers pressed against the windows, gazing at the fleeting landscape. I wondered where they came from and prayed they returned heroes.

Every day I saw more and more troops and tanks and armors rumbling by the house. I waved at the soldiers, and some waved back. Many were no more than eighteen, heading for battle, some never to return. I wanted to hop on one of the trains and travel with them. Side by side, we could win the war together. I wasn't quite sure what America was fighting about, but I knew we were the good guys.

As I grew older, the troop trains stopped, the weary soldiers returned, and the haunting whistles of my inquisitive youth faded like invisible ink. Little did I know that ten years later, I would be on a troop train heading not to a battle zone, but to a tour of duty as an Army paratrooper at Fort Campbell, Kentucky. Later I would start a twenty-five-year newspaper career.

I would write about wars, spaceships, presidents, sports figures, movie stars, murders, and history. Like my immigrant relatives before me, I would live my dream, not to the pounding sound of a railroad jackhammer or amid the smell of a smoked-filled foundry, but to the melodious tapping of a typewriter creating my paradise.

Chapter 3
Little Chicago

Violence is the last refuge of the incompetent.
—Isaac Asimov

A frigid winter wind whipped through the streets of Olean. The strong wind almost knocked Italian immigrant Louis Veno off his feet. With his eyebrows covered with snow and his nose displaying a purple tint, his appearance transformed into a much older twenty-two-year-old.

A gray wool cap wrapped tightly over his head and ears, and a thin, blazing red bandanna covered his mouth. He exhaled and inhaled through the cloth like an intense operating room surgeon. He gave little attention to the blizzard.

Louis's mind was in overload with an urgency more important than the bitter, January 1920 weather. This freezing Italian immigrant needed a job, any job. He pondered over and over the places he had to visit to ask, or even beg for work. With his head down, he gazed at the shifting snow. A sense of desperation hit—where to turn next? Without a firm destination, he moved aimlessly through the streets, knocking on every shop door and factory seeking even one day's work. His money dwindled and he was running out of time. He lived alone and had only a few days before the rent was due on his one-room apartment. His father, Carlo, lived close by in a tiny house and had no money to give his son. It was hard times and everyone carried on alone.

"I would pay anyone who had a tip on a job one dollar. That was a lot of money in those days," my father recalled.

After searching with in vain for work, he called an old friend and with a stroke of luck finally got a good bite.

"There's a dairy farm outside of town," the friend told him. "You have to walk about five miles. It's called Yehl's. The owner is looking for someone to milk the cows, clean out the stable, and shovel snow around the barns. It pays about four dollars. You may find a couple of days work there. I just heard about the job a few hours ago."

Milking cows? It was not one of his skills, but he was going to learn on the job. "I'm not going to wait until tomorrow. I'll walk over there today."

He made the right decision. Louis landed a couple of days work. That would be enough to keep him going for a while.

It was January 17, 1920; a day Western New York and the rest of America would change its drinking habits. It was the day Prohibition went into effect. The government decided Americans should stop drinking alcohol. "The Volstead Act," as it was called officially, would dry up the country. At least, that's what the politicians in Washington thought.

While my father gave the little thought to the new law, others saw Prohibition as an opportunity to climb out of the bowels of poverty and make plenty of money. Only the most cynical or the most hopeful believed that people were going to stop drinking because the law said so.

A hundred dry laws won't avert a man's thirst for a cold beer, a shot of whiskey or a highball, many reasoned.

A new business emerged across the nation—selling bootleg booze.

Overnight, moonshine stills sprang up everywhere. Thousands of peep-hole speakeasies followed. Their window shades were drawn and the doors were locked, and there was plenty of live action inside. Illegal booze could be found for sale in house parlors and grocery store back rooms. With enough bribe money, you could have a dazzling nightclub like the Sunset Inn a few miles outside of Olean, which was run by a small-time thug called "Buffalo" Al Ritchie.

The country took on a new adventure: romantic trips to secret hideaways to drink 'til dawn, listen to hot music, and dance the night away. Americans loved it.

Swept in with the illegal gin, whiskey, and rum came the Jazz Age. New hot songs were written. Singers like the Jazz Age Sweetheart, Ruth Etting, sang "Button up Your Overcoat," "Ten Cents a Dance," and "Mean to Me." Plenty of work waited for singers, bands, and bartenders.

Chicago was the capitol of the bootleg era, and Al Capone was a self-proclaimed Chairman of the Board. His tentacles reached all over the United States. Rumors had it that he once stopped in Olean while on his way to Chicago. Someone said they spotted "Scarface" at the Erie train station one night.

"Stayed at the hotel across the street," a retired railroad engineer recalled. "He threw money around like it was water."

The story was never substantiated. Like Elvis, Capone was spotted all over. Ironically, Elliott Ness, the man who helped put Capone out of business and in prison, lived 30 miles away from Olean. The Department of Treasury agent, this "Untouchable" crime fighter, died after going bankrupt in a lumber business in Coudersport, Pennsylvania, in the 1940s. A meeting between the two in western New York was highly unlikely.

Whiskey was distilled in western Pennsylvania in the late 1800s because farmers were looking for more ways to profit from their grain. In the 1920s, whiskey, pure white from the still and aged in barrels, would prove to be the most sought-after drink in America. The demand was so great that anyone who could gather the ingredients and concoct whiskey could set up a shop illegally and make a good living. Some of the Olean speakeasies had names such as "The Bucket of Blood," "Bull Dog's," "The Copper Teakettle," "The Silver Stove Pipe" and "Black Hand Mary's."

Trouble brewed when the competition got rough and gunfights broke out for territories. The Olean-Bradford area got the name

"Little Chicago" because of bloodshed and countless murders. Seventy miles from Olean was the Canadian border, an important link to alcohol traffic in the United States.

In *The Great Illusion*, author Herbert Asbury compared the illegal alcohol boat traffic from Canada at the port of Bridgeburg, on the Niagara River near Buffalo, to a traffic jam in New York City. The boats loaded with thousand of cases of alcohol were taken to the American side and unloaded a few yards from the United States Customs office. Bribing custom officers was so widespread that it was impossible to find an officer who didn't have his hand out.

Seventy-five miles away, "Little Chicago" was emerging. The smell of big money from peddling alcohol reached the noses of a few ambitious young Italian immigrants living there. As their appetites for money grew, a mob war erupted between the Olean thugs and the Bradford hoods. Twenty murders went unsolved between those small cities during the bootleg days, not to mention the dozens that were solved.

The same rules used today for drug war killings applied during the period of Little Chicago. Move in on someone else's territory, and the encroacher ran the risk of getting blown away. My parents kept me on the edge of my kitchen chair talking about those insane days in the neighborhood. They were unclear on many of the details, but I understood what happened. As my father and mother talked, I heard history unfolding. When they failed to tell me about the violence because of my age, my imagination took over.

The criminals—these misfits—tried to intimidate the honest, hardworking Italians. "A mob figure tried to shake me down," my father said. In my version, I was the one who proved to be as tough as those young thugs. They never bothered my father or our family again. Pa was not a crusader, but his song rang out: "Leave me and mine in peace."

Like today, many people knew about the murders, but would never speak about them publicly. In private quarters, the gossipers whispered and pointed fingers, but always while looking over their shoulders. The wrong ears might be listening. Revenge and retaliation played a strong role in keeping civil-minded people quiet.

The Bradford-Olean area teemed with gunfire like the Wild West—a western range war without the cattle. One chilling story I heard repeated time after time gave me a frightening perception of how violent the times were. Two thugs chased a man in daylight hours down 4th Street and Forrest Avenue, an Olean residential area. The man ran for his life across the street. He tripped over a wire fence in front of the corner house and fell helpless on the seeded lawn.

The hoodlums walked up to him. While he lay on the grass, the killers pumped about four slugs in his head. Blood splattered over the sidewalk. They kicked him a few times, and then walked away without a sound. The murdered man was identified as Anthony Minniti, a 34-year-old Italian from New Jersey. Minniti's murderers were never found.

Mob killings did not exclude women. My parents told me of a woman who was killed, mutilated, wrapped in wire, and thrown in a sack, then dropped at the city dump. It was a scary and crazy time. Even as a kid, the little bit I picked up played around in my head.

The Olean gang shot at the Bradford gang and visa versa. Then everyone shot wildly at everyone else. Terrible marksmen, the shooters seldom hit the target. One out of ten shootouts ended in death, an incredibly low percentage. The low score even gave gun manufacturers a bad name.

"These guys were so bad they made *The Gang Who Couldn't Shoot Straight* look like a bunch of sharp shooters," a citizen commented. Eventually, imported hit men corrected the miscues. When the scores improved and the gun smoke cleared, the number of widows increased.

Although many of the murders involved illegal booze territories, jealous lovers wiped out other individuals. Various relatives of the victims still live in the area. A descendant here and there will talk about the events, others will not.

One of the local murder trials crawled onto the pages of *The Tiger at the Bar* by Chester Harris. The book is a colorful and adventurous story of a great American trial lawyer, Charles Margiotti, of Pittsburgh. Margiotti, who handled over two hundred murder cases in his brilliant career, claims that not one of his clients died in the electric chair. A few spent their natural lives behind bars, but none ever received the death penalty. The lawyer carried that track record with pride, which people picked up from his walk and tilt of his head.

Among the highly publicized murder trials that *Tiger at the Bar* details was a mob hit by two local thugs. They were charged with killing an Olean businessman. The murder trial took place in late summer of 1928 in Little Valley, New York, about sixteen miles from Olean, the county seat where court business was conducted.

Frank Femia and Thomas Del Giudice, two small-time hoods, were charged with the murder of Joe Scutella, a local merchant who sold groceries in the front of the store. Rumors ran wild about his selling alcoholic beverages in the back room. The murder appeared to stem from a gang war. Newspapers reported that Scutella was found by a farmer along the Allegheny River, a few miles from Olean, with this head slashed and his right ear severed, a racket-killing trademark. Returning the ear to the mob boss was proof that the job was completed.

The Scutella shooting proved once again to be sloppy work by the ruthless but amateur thugs. They removed his ear, but forgot to check his pulse.

When they left the butchered grocer on the riverbank, he was still alive. Jack Dempsey, famous Olean Police Chief, sat at his bedside when the man identified his assailants before he died.

Although District Attorney Krieger's case was flimsy, he charged both Femia and Del Giudice. The DA clung to a thread of evidence that affirmed a "dying declaration" as enough, based on the rationale that a dying man, to save his soul, will always tell the truth.

Margiotti tore the argument apart, stating that the declaration was a lie invented to frame the two accused. He discredited the dead man's daughter, Mary, who made an attempt to introduce this evidence. Her plea failed, and three hours later, the two were found not guilty. Dempsey was never called to the stand. After the trial, killings around "Little Chicago" went into full swing again and continued for the remainder of Prohibition.

Talk of the Scutella murder circled the area for years. His murderer escaped the noose, although the loudest buzz claimed that a small-time thug named Al Ritchie had knowledge of the slaying of the grocer, and he may have been responsible for dozens of murders in the Olean-Bradford area. Ritchie, an import from Buffalo, owned Sunset Inn, a restaurant outside of Olean.

Incredible as it may seem, he was also a special investigator for the DA's office. He used his gold badge to get rid of competitors until DA Kreiger decided to yank his credentials and get rid of Ritchie. Femia was killed a few weeks later. His killer was never discovered and the murders went on and on with few suspects or arrests.

On a warm afternoon of June 5, 1931, Ritchie sat in his car parked on River Street in Bradford. He had just lit a cigarette and was relaxing in the driver's seat when a man walked up to the front open window and pumped six slugs into Ritchie's head. He died the next day in the Bradford hospital. After several attempts on his life, the mob finally succeeded and ended the life of an outlaw who enjoyed fancy clothes, expensive cars, and gold badges.

Dempsey walked a balancing act during the mob war. He didn't want any of the killings in his jurisdiction, so he decided to step into the Scutella murder. Despite his tough talk, the Irish cop did little to stop most of the bloodshed. More often, he let the gangsters kill each other.

The majority were young Italian thugs killing young Italian thugs. Dempsey couldn't care less. A direct threat to his personal credentials, however, aroused his fury. Although he wasn't known to be a crooked cop, he apparently loved to decide who was in and who was out. His ego matched his personal power. Nothing moved without Dempsey's sanction. If anyone ran a speakeasy, it was because Dempsey let it remain open.

Later in his long career, in the 1930s, he gave Pat Dawson, a lifelong close friend and small-time bookie, the green light to run a betting parlor in the middle of downtown Olean. Dawson, a well-liked and generous Irishman, earned well over one hundred million dollars at that location. Friends help friends.

The murders more or less ended when Prohibition did. When Dempsey died in the late 1960s, the Jazz Age, Prohibition, and the mob were long gone. Only Dawson remained. Dawson, who went to church every day of his adult life, gave thousands of dollars to charity, to priests, and almost anyone who asked him.

Dawson helped Ted Marchibroda, a National Football League coach for the Buffalo Bills in the 1980s, launch his football career. Marchibroda, an Oil City, Pennsylvania, football star, got a full scholarship to St. Bonaventure University with a lot of help from Dawson, who was known to be charitable to the university.

"Ted never forgot Pat," said an old friend. "Marchibroda would visit Dawson every time he was in Olean." Dawson died in his late eighties in a nursing home. And with him died the last link to the city's bootleg days. Dawson's betting parlor, which was nearly as big as a modern-day Wal-Mart store, vanished from the center of the city. It was replaced by a pharmacy.

Chapter 4
Internment Camps for
Italians and Germans

"America had internment camps not only for Japanese, but for Italian and German aliens during World War II," recalled my grandfather, Carlo Veno. "I am talking about Italians who were loyal and who had lived in this country for 40 years."

It was the summer of 1949, and he was reminiscing about the years of the war and his fears of those unsettling times for Italian Americans. Sitting on his favorite walnut rocker on the back porch, he spoke to me in almost incomprehensible broken English about the treatment of Italians during war. I was a young boy then, and the full impact of what he was saying was mostly lost on me at the time. All I understood was his coming to America had shaped my life. As young as I was, I liked to listen to him. I wanted to know everything about him for my heritage and future.

The internment story came up as he spoke of federal agents moving around his neighborhood in Olean, New York, in 1942, yanking shortwave equipment away from Italians living there.

"The FBI knocked on the door and asked me if I had any contact with people in Italy," he recalled. "I told them I have a son over there and I listen to Italian music on the shortwave radio.

"They came into the house, pulled out the shortwave, and asked if I had any cameras, photos, and guns around the house. I said no and they left.

"I heard friends and fellow workers on the railroad say that the government was placing Italians in camps on the West Coast and relocating them away from the ocean shoreline.

"I thought maybe they were going to put us in jail until after the war because we never became citizens," he said with a pained look, fine lines wrinkling around his eyes and forehead.

It was vague to me then, but later in life and after much research, I found out that in this great country during World War II, panic spread in Washington. Concerns about the infiltration of spies reached a paranoia level. The government moved to detain and relocate—without a hearing—Japanese in America, and also some Italians and Germans.

While the tragedy involving Japanese-American relocation has become well-known, few Americans are aware of the relocation program that forced thousands of Italians and Germans in California to leave their homes for so-called "security safe zones."

In his remarkable book, *Unknown Internment,* Professor Stephen Fox of Humboldt State University in Arcata, California, revealed that Italians and Germans had been relocated from their homes near the shoreline of the Pacific Ocean and interned at Fort Missoula in Montana. Italian fishermen were banned from netting and their boats were seized. These were aliens who had lived in America for 40 years, who were loyal to America with sons in the US Army. Suddenly, they were harassed and interned because they had never obtained US citizenship. What was staggering was that half the Italians in the United States in 1942—millions—were aliens. Why? For reasons ranging from illiteracy to complacency, many did not become citizens. When the war broke out, the Italian aliens were put into the potential-enemy category.

President Franklin Roosevelt ordered the arrest of all Italian and German aliens who were thought to be a danger to American security after America entered World War II. On the West Coast, it was estimated that a half million aliens were living there. Many were relocated to the interior of California until the war was over. More well-known was the fate of the Japanese-Americans, who were interned in racetracks and camps until after the war.

Author Fox, who spent countless hours researching government records, states that the most persistent advocate of internment for aliens was War Department General John L. Dewitt. A man with little combat experience, Dewitt pushed for Italian and German aliens to be interned simultaneously with Japanese-Americans. Had Dewitt prevailed, tens of thousands of German and Italian aliens would have been interned, causing an even greater domestic crisis.

Fox believes that what happened to Italians and Germans in 1942 was part of the dress rehearsal for the McCarthy purge of the 1950s, precisely because in this case, the aliens were targeted not for racial but for ideological reasons. It was an obsession with national security.

After France fell to the Germans in 1942, panic increased to the point that even fishermen like Giuseppe DiMaggio, father of baseball's Yankee Clipper, Joe DiMaggio, was banned from working on Fisherman's Wharf in San Francisco and could not eat in his son's restaurant. Mr. DiMaggio came to America in 1898, had nine children, all of them American citizens. The insanity stopped as the war came to an end. Few, if any, disloyal Italians were found. Most had sons in the armed services, and many died for the country they loved.

After the war, the Japanese received much deserved reparations while the Italian and Germans were forgotten, the records buried in government repositories. There are a few movements for reparations, but with nonexistent results to date.

Chapter 5
The Old Rugged Church

The thick pinewood benches in the dimly-lit, one-room church added to the dreary coldness. I shivered.

How could an eight-year-old sleep during Sunday night services?

Lying on my back, with my ankle-long coat up pulled up over my nose to keep me warm, I could barely see the ceiling above me. It was a miracle that the wooden beams kept the shaky roof together.

How could I ever forget those services in the winter of 1940, especially the sounds and voices that came out of that handful of Congregationalists inside Brother Ross's Four Square Church on Maple Street in Olean, New York? While the freezing winter winds rattled the shingles outside the church, inside, Brother Ross played a familiar hymn on the piano and preached about the Lord. The worshipers, both arms above their heads, fingers shaking, looked upward at that beamed ceiling. "Praise the Lord," the worshipers shouted, their words punctuated by a frequent "amen." Probably, they listened to their own voices and not the preacher's words.

My father was always among the ten or fifteen parishioners who attended every Sunday. It was a small group, but vocal enough to make sure God could hear them.

As an impetuous and impatient youngster, I thought the night services were endless and torturous. For Pa's sake, I would squirm around as little as possible under my coat. It was usually my luck to get a squeaky bench. Today I think of those nights as beautiful and spiritual memories.

One night my father, Luigi, as he like to be called because it was so Italian, stood next to me with bowed head and eyes closed. With both hands fluttering in the air, he thanked his God for his new and welcome blessing. He'd found a job.

Luigi was a handsome, well-built forty-year-old Italian immigrant. He was short, with jet-black hair and deep blue eyes— that's the way I saw Pa. I stared in awe at this rugged but gentle man praying in English and then in Italian

"God understands all languages," he said.

I stayed quiet, still a shivering mess of misery. I wondered if God knew how cold it was in Brother Ross's church. The heat from the coal-burning potbelly stove in the middle of church did not radiate enough heat to keep me from trembling, despite my heavy coat and boots. After stretching out on the bench for what seemed like forever, I sat up and put my coat on.

The marathon services lasted two to three hours, so after the first hour I once again gave way to the hard benches and dozed off.

I learned very little about salvation then, but I learned a lot about my father, about his perseverance, his courage, and his deep religious belief. I did not understand what he meant when he said that one had to be "born again and saved" to reach Paradise. However, his faith and his indomitable courage to weather life's rugged storms did rub off on me. The words "can't" and "impossible" were removed from Pa's dictionary.

My father left the Catholic Church because he couldn't feel heaven's energy among Catholics. At that time the Mass was said in Latin, which added to his confusion and uncertainty about his faith. He also objected to confessing his sins to another person. "I need no interceder," he said. "What I have to confess is between God and me."

Eventually, he left the Catholic Church when he met Rose and Joe, who persuaded him to go an Evangelical church, or in those days, what was called a "Holy Roller" church. After joining the group, Pa took a great deal of verbal harassment at work and around town.

"Louis has gone insane and become a follower of the weirdos," a neighbor told my mother.

"It was as if he was struck by lightning," another neighbor commented.

His life did take an upturn. The job he found during the post-Depression period paid big money—five dollars a day for ten hours of work.

What a blessing. He was in the "clover." My dad would have enough to take care of his family and heavenly obligations. The collection plate at Brother Ross's house of worship overflowed.

Thus, Luigi Veno, who arrived at Ellis Island at age 15 with an immigrant tag around his neck and clutching his young sister Mary Grace's hand, was living the American dream. After escaping the punishing poverty of his Italian homeland, he would never be hungry again.

"It was all the Lord's doing," he said. "And what more can one ask for?"

My mother, Anna, an astute businesswoman, refused to agree that Pa's newfound wealth resulted from his changed spiritual belief, but she tolerated it and invested his money. She remained a Catholic. With my father's earnings growing each day, she raised five children, and also bought houses in New York and Florida.

My brother, Tony, and I switched from one church to another, but we ended up practicing Catholics. My father constantly urged us to go his church, and at times we did. However, since all childhood friends were Catholics, Tony and I stayed Catholics. Nonetheless, I carried a great deal of my father's beliefs with me through life.

As a child, I was hurt and wondered why many people disliked "The Holy Rollers." I didn't realize that the entire town was divided into Catholics and mainstream Protestants. Anything that was not quite either was foreign and weird. "They are trying to change our Bible." The words echoed over and over in our town. The animosity against them lingered a long time before it cooled down.

One Sunday night, half-asleep at Brother's Ross's church, I rested my head on those hard benches, and waited for my father to say those welcoming words, "It's time to go." Instead, I was startled by earth shaking and frightening noises coming from the church walls. I jumped up and thought the world was coming to an end. Quickly, I pulled on my father's suit sleeve.

"Pa, what's going on?" I said. I could see the plasterboard on the walls shaking.

"It's a gang of local kids beating on the wall," my father said. He remained calm as he put his hand around my shoulder and pulled me closer to him.

"Holy Rollers, Holy Rollers, hit the road, go away," the voices screamed loud enough to be heard inside the church.

I ran to the door, opened it slightly, and peeked out for a look at them. They were a couple of big, rough neighborhood guys and a few small ones about my age. I knew them. The next day I looked for the one kid my size and punched him in the mouth.

He looked surprised. "Hey, what did I do?"

"Don't disturb a place of worship," I said. "Besides, you woke me up."

After that encounter, the noise stopped. The word got around that some of the "Holy Rollers" weren't turning the other cheek.

A few years later my brother and I stopped going to that church and started blending with the Catholics. My father continued to go faithfully every Sunday.

Years later, I drove by Brother Ross' church. When I glanced over to see it again, the rush of cherished memories surfaced. These times were emotional and moving. For me, the reminiscences represented an important repository of my childhood, stuffed with treasured recollections of my father.

Even today, decades later, when I return to Olean to see my brother and friends, I never forget to take that drive by the church. Although time has changed many things—the neighborhood, the worshipers, and the city—the church incredibly remains the same. Sunday night services continue.

The outside needs some repairs. The roof and the sidewalk could do with patching up. Yet the church remains intact—like a giant, unmovable rock. Its brown, faded shingles still look the same to me as they did when an eight-year-old child shivered inside.

I long to go inside the church again, and glance at part of my childhood. Maybe one day, I will. To run my hand gently across those bumpy pinewood benches where my father and I sat close together on those Sunday nights would set free the past ghosts of those precious memories, which would allow me to relive my joyful age of innocence.

Chapter 6
The Park Bench Gang

I remember my youth and the feelings that will never
come back anymore—the feeling that I could last
forever, outlast the sea, the earth, and all men.
                    —Joseph Conrad

"Early impressions are hard to eradicate," Saint Jerome wrote.
"When once wool has been dyed purple, who can restore it to its
previous whiteness?"

With childhood friends we remain rooted in our unmovable
recollection of them. To each other we never grow up. We age but
never change. We saw each other as we did when we sat together
on the park benches in Boardman Park, draped in Army and Navy
fatigues, enjoying the hot, lazy summer days. We were seventeen
and enjoying our last fling at youth's exciting, crazy times.
Having the confidence of young bulls running down matadors, we
rushed into to any venture that was thrilling, dangerous, and
laughable.

One of most enterprising and unpredictable guys in the gang was
Anthony "Mize" Marra. Mize and I joined the Army paratroopers.
While at Fort Campbell, Kentucky, he obtained a couple of live hand
grenades.

"When I get back home, I'll get some guys together, and we'll
blow the grenades up in the park," said the laughing, dark haired,
thin-built Mize.

While on furlough on a cold Christmas Eve in 1953, this

47

seventeen-year-old paratrooper passed the word around that he would toss a grenade in a pond north of the city. Some of the guys were skeptical until they saw the baseball-size metal ball with a pin on it in Mize's hand, with Mize waving it around.

"He's got to be nuts," one of the guys said.

"Naw, just big balls," another Park Bencher remarked.

Like John Wayne on the movie battlefield, Mize got in his kneeling position to throw the live grenade in the air.

"Make sure you pull the pin and toss it quickly over the bank. I don't want it to blow up in your face," screamed one of the guys.

"I know what I'm doing," said a cocky Mize, who tossed it over a frozen pond as the rest of the guys watched from a safe distance.

There was loud sound, a flash in the sky, and the ground shook like a slight earthquake. The smell of gunpowder permeated the air.

A huge roar and cheer came out of the guys. If the cops had come by that day, the downtown jail would have been overflowing with Park Bench guys.

I never knew what Mize did with the other grenade. Years later he told me he buried it somewhere in the Polly Wise hills north of the city. I never asked where. As nutty as it was, it was hilarious.

The fifties were the age of radio, pinball machines, pool halls, wax lips, *The Green Hornet*, and *The Shadow*. It was a time before gays came out of the closet. It was a time when the prejudiced considered Jews Communists, blacks inferior, Irish either cops or drunks, Italians mobsters, and Polish uneducated. White Protestants were the elite, lived in Seneca Heights and had all the good jobs. The Anglo-Saxons ruled.

Members of the Park Bench Gang were sons of middle class blue-collar workers. The group included Germans, Irish, Italians, French, Eastern Europeans, and Arabs. Although we sat on the bench together, we were subdivided into ethic groups in our neighborhoods. The Italians lived in one neighborhood, the Polish in another; the Irish scattered around the city and blacks in a small, isolated area, similar to the situation in a lot of

American cities.

It was a remarkable group of young men, who eventually were lifted to a professional level their parents could only dream about. Their fathers' fate was to know only the noise and smell of burning metal from Clark Brothers' foundry, pounding of spikes on the Erie and Pennsylvania railroads, and agony of living on your knees eight hours a day setting tile.

Their sons would be doctors, lawyers, judges, teachers, millionaire businessmen, chefs, music producers, newspaper reporters and editors, restaurant owners. Others would follow in their parents' footsteps and work in the local factories under better conditions. They would marry, have children, leave their neighborhood, and live in the suburbs. Others would leave and move far away, returning only on a holiday. Outside of a reunion every five years, we seldom communicate, but mere glances of old friends connect us to youthful and joyful memories.

I can still hear the sounds of baseballs cracking into the summer skies. I can smell the fresh summer grass, and the voices clamoring and chatting about the war, politics, sports, girls, jobs, and the future.

Shooting fireworks in the summer sounds like mild entertainment, but the fireworks caused real problems to us when the police got furious and decided to crack down, making the summer a real hell for us.

The park was close to the creek and we built a houseboat to swim off and move around the water. At night we launched fireworks from a bazooka-type pipe on a creek bank and sent them zooming across the creek into the sky. The cops came around almost every night, but we were elusive until one night the sky fell in.

The guys had to swim across the Olean Creek as the police were shooting holes in the houseboat. After a frantic chase, guys like Billy "Bugs" Fote and Dick "Zon" Aiello, got a taste of police gunfire in the darkness and a night in jail. The overnight jail visit slowed the fun down, but never stopped it.

Before moving on in life, I shared many memorable moments on the park bench. Saturday afternoon sandlot football gave us time to smash each other in the face. We sat on the benches drinking quarts of beer that we brought from Ralph's supermarket across the street. We even attempted to have an indoor feast.

Franny Fote came up with a bright idea to cook pigeons and drink his father's red wine as a get-together meal. The not-so-gourmet dinner was enough to make some of us so sick that we could have been hospitalized. Franny grew up to be a physician and we let him concentrate on medicine while someone else planned meals.

When the police continued to harass at the park, we decided to have some fun with the cops.

"Let's go and set fireworks off behind the police station. The rockets will go off directly over the roof. The noise will scare the shit out of them," said Louie DiMarino. "I made a long wax wick that'll give us an enough time to be miles away before the fireworks go off."

Why we wanted to set off fireworks over the police station doesn't make any sense today, but at seventeen it was daring, exciting, and fun. As we sat on the park bench, the police patrol car slowly went by. The police looked at us almost puzzled. They knew something was wrong, but couldn't figure out what.

We outsmarted the cops. When you are young, you do anything crazy. With a bunch of guys, you will do even wackier things.

In later years, Harry McGavish, the founder of the Park Bench reunions and a former schoolteacher, never drifted far from the park benches in the summer time. He picked up a bargain beer from Ralph's supermarket across from the park and relaxed on the bench. Vince, his brother, a half-foot shorter, was also a former teacher. Vince was an exceptional athlete in baseball and football, but passed up college sports. He settled down to married life and moved away.

We all had nicknames, like Pump Handle, Mize, Chico, Bugs, Noodles, Hoppy, Gusty, LuBean, and Bo. There was John "The Snake" Augustine, Tony "Junny" Bassano, Bobby "Saur" Wise, Evo

"Monk" Malpeidi, Jimmy "Nippy" Napoleon. Everyone had a nickname except Bob Steiger. I never knew why. They called me Trigger. A neighbor of mine, Neil Connolly, tagged me with the name and it stuck.

Why Trigger? He just picked it out of the air, like with most of the nicknames.

One of the oddest guys who came around the park was Nick "Pizazz" Platter. An older, squat guy, Nick was an ex-fighter who married a woman half his age and trouble. She had a bad habit of getting locked in the movies every Friday night. At least that is what she would tell Nick on Saturday morning. Finally Nick got wind that she was sleeping with younger guys and a small war broke out. Nick, about the size of Mickey Rooney, punched his wife. One night she packed her bags and left him.

Nick sat around and cried about her. "I miss her so much." Nick was never the same, and some say he may have died of a broken heart.

There was a time one of the guys, Tommy Sirianni, was shot with a rifle by a good neighbor for pulling a few plums from a tree. Tommy survived without side effects.

Others climbed the professional ladder with little education. Francis "Hoppy" Caya, a high school dropout, would buy a restaurant, "Red and Trudy's," and go on to be a successful entrepreneur. The restaurant still has some of the tastiest hamburgers in Western New York.

I think about guys like "Pump Handle" Kisel, whose brother George lost a leg hopping freight trains. I understand Pump Handle is a pig farmer making a good living and enjoying every minute.

The most energetic guy I knew was Joe "Grease" De Rose. We both worked on Crosby's milk truck as kids, getting up at 4 a.m. before going to school. We got ten dollars a week and all the milk we could take home. I left the job for a pin-setting job at the bowling alley while Joe stayed on.

Joe loved to work with his hands. Although Joe went on to college, he had a change of heart and decided to go to work for his brother-in-law as a sheet metal worker and became the president and major owner of the company. The last time I saw Joe, he was content, but looked a little pale. I found out later he had colon cancer and died a few years later. It's a shame when you work as hard as Joe and are denied a moment of rest and retirement.

Another one of the Park Bench guys whose life was cut short in his prime was Louie Mara. Louie's parents, hard working Italians, lived a few blocks from my house. Louie, a clean-living guy, always looked for an opportunity to work for himself.

After a tiring job as coffee salesmen with Continental Coffee Company, he decided to open a deli. With the help of a doctor friend, Louie put some money together and opened a downtown deli. Louie had a knack for spotting skilled people. He hired the area's top chef, John Cappelletti, who helped Louie become an instant success. Louie's wife, Mary Barbara, who kept a watchful eye on Louie's finances, was also a driving force in his success. His wife once called the police to raid the barbershop I owned because Louie was losing too much money playing poker there. We didn't get raided, but Louie stopped playing poker. He played for bigger stakes in the restaurant world.

One, hard cold winter night, a gas pipe exploded in the deli basement and the resulting fire leveled the building. The insurance money helped Louie build his dream restaurant. It's called "The Old Library." The elegant restaurant and inn got rave reviews. That's as good as it gets in Western New York. Louie was on his way to achieving his dream.

Then one hot summer afternoon, the dream turned into a nightmare. Louie decided to get some exercise and took a sixteen-mile bike ride to his summer place at Cuba Lake. An apparent fatal heart attack shattered the blossoming career of this self-made entrepreneur. Although his wife and children carried on the dream, I always wondered what it would be like if Louie were still around.

Probably the richest members of the Park Bench Gang were the Dwaileebes. John and Charlie took over their father Jim's Pepsi Cola distributorship when the business was in terrible financial shape.

After years of struggling, the franchise took off and the Dwaileebes with it. Charles eventually sold out, retired in Arizona and died. Johnny kept all the stock, then sold the franchise for millions.

Not all of the guys enjoyed financial success, but they were part of my rich past and made my youth an enjoyable adventure.

As youth fled, the Park Bench Gang went their separate ways, destined to meet years later at reunions.

New faces have taken over the park and few sit on the green benches. No one swims in the creek anymore. A small basketball court in the middle of the park draws the attention of the younger set. Only memories and the ghosts of the past hover on summer nights.

I closed my eyes and saw a deep green, perfectly straight row of maple trees lining the park with the magnificent splendor of the past shining down on the young Park Bench Gang. A whistling cool breeze blew the tree leaves symmetrically sideways, releasing strange sounds, voices, chattering and ghosts dancing on the matching green park benches.

I heard the clash of football helmets, the crack of baseballs ringing throughout the summer air, and the loud splash of water from swimmers in the creek nearby.

The park benches were occupied with guys waving their hands and drinking cheap beer. A convertible with a bunch of kids from the other side of town flew down North Union Street, a few feet from the park benches.

"Slow the damn car," shouted young Harry McGavish, shaking his fist at the speeding car.

Across the street on the second-floor porch above a grocery store, Jeep Sirianni, sitting on a worn-out living room couch, barefoot and bare-chested, shouted at the top of his lungs: "Give 'em hell, Harry. These young shits are all the same. They ain't got no respect for anything."

In the middle of the park, Dicky Aiello, Bugs Fote and Phil Belvees were putting a silver chromium pipe beer can launcher together. It looked like a homemade bazooka.

"Put the fireworks in first and drop a can in and watch them sail across the creek," said Dicky.

Over in the baseball diamond, Bobby Weis was in a Joe DiMaggio stance as Evo Malpiedi fired down the worn-thin hardball with Joe De Rose, Johnny Karowitz, Hoppy Caya, and LuBean Veno in the outfield.

Sitting on another bench was Harry, Lou DiMarino, and Franny Fote discussing the future of something meaningless. A few feet away, Jimmy "Noodles" strummed on a small banjo singing "Ramona" as Jimmy and Charlie Dwaileebe, along with Dicky Fote, sang along.

A mail truck drove by, and Jimmy "Nippy" Napoleon stuck his head out the window and shouted, "See you guys later."

On the other side of the park, Vince McGavish and Johnny Degolier were talking about high school football. Johnny Augustini and Tony Bassano were getting ready to go to the Castle Restaurant and learn the trade as chefs.

We were young and full energy and fun. We thought those days of hot summer in the park would never end. We just kept having fun. No one reminded us the fun would be over soon, like youth, fleeting too fast, never to return.

I walked home and in the distance I saw my mother, dressed in a red flowered dress with her apron on, and my father next to her with his gray work pants and green short-sleeve shirt and his felt hat cocked to the right on his head. They were laughing and teasing each other like they always did.

My mother smiled and saw me.

"You're late for dinner, but I saved yours—it's in the oven.

"You have to learn how important time is," she said with a broad smile that lit up her beautiful face. My father and mother held hands, looked back, both smiled again and vanished down the hallway.

The sun seemed to remain in the sky longer than ever. Suspended in the heavens, it refused to go down that day. When I opened my eyes again, the sounds and voices vanished, all that remained were the ghosts dancing and gliding across the green grass of the park.

Chapter 7
Dull Shears

Who is rich? He that is content.
—Benjamin Franklin

I never believed in the worn-out catch phrase, "If you want to know who your friends are, go in business."

Although I have the best friends anyone could ever want, most never patronized me as a barber. They would do anything for me except let me cut their hair. I was a great guy with dull shears. They often dropped into the barbershop to talk to me, but would always ask for John McNarney, the barber in the next chair, to cut their hair.

Others would patronize Ray Padlo, an outstanding haircutter, and brilliant entrepreneur. Ray, a high school football star, parlayed an overwhelmingly successful barber business into twenty or more income properties, a salon with a dozen employees and assets well over a million dollars.

Since my popularity did not help my wages, I sought other income by picking up a few bucks playing poker in the back room and working as a bartender. Unfulfilled, I wanted something more rewarding in life.

Between working my extra jobs and attending St. Bonaventure University, I was spending my free time pounding on an old, beaten typewriter, attempting to write marketable short stories.

At that time, nothing seemed challenging. While the room air conditioner was buzzing over my head in the barbershop, I sat in the barber's chair staring out the window, looking at a dismal future.

And then it happened.

"A phone call at the dry cleaners for you, Carl," said George Gayton, a presser. It was probably my wife, I thought, who wanted me to pick up baby food for our daughter. "I will be right there." I buttoned up my white smock and walked out of the barbershop and went next door.

Angie and Tony Petrucelli owned a dry cleaning store next door, and I always used their phone. The barbershop could not afford one. Angie and Tony were lifelong friends and a generous couple. They had two sons, John, a good friend of mine, and Tom. John was a lawyer who spent every free moment at the racetrack. We both burned a lot of money betting the horses, but we had a lot of expensive fun.

I thanked George and picked up the phone. "Hello. Carl Veno speaking," I said.

A very Southern voice came back at me. "Please hold for Mr. McGee."

Who the hell is Mr. McGee? Maybe a bill collector, or a goofy salesman, I thought.

Then it hit me. McGee was the editor of the *Orlando Sentinel,* the one Elba, my father's friend in Miami, had mentioned. After being put on hold for almost a minute, I heard this strong, deep voice,

My heart pounded a thousand beats per minute.

"Carl, my name is Wilson McGee. Elba Luisi sent me your resume. She thinks you might make a good sportswriter. I know your background in writing is limited, but your sports experience could come in handy. I understand you did some prize fighting and we could use some of that courage down here. We're in a newspaper war with Gannett. I need some reporters in Brevard County. Are you interested?"

"Yes, I am." I answered without hesitating.

"Of course, you may be called on to write other news stories, but we can help you with that." He added, "I generally use the personnel department to call in applicants, but since Elba and I are such good friends, I decided to do this myself. How does it all sound?"

I was numb. I could barely believe what I heard. "Great," I said as I cleared my dry throat.

"How soon can you get down here to take some testing and talk to our personnel department?"

"Like yesterday," I said.

"Good," he said. "We will see you here next Tuesday at 2 o'clock. As soon as your airline tickets are confirmed, call the personnel department and tell them your arrival time. And expect to stay a couple of days for orientation. Nice talking to you, Carl. See you next week."

"Thank you, Mr. McGee. I'm so grateful to have this opportunity."

"It's going to be a lot of hard work for you, but I'm sure you can do it."

My mind made a swift transition from being nearly an unemployed barber and writing rejected short stories, to a full-time working reporter for the *Orlando Sentinel* in Cocoa Beach, Florida, at the Kennedy Space Center. It was beyond my wildest dreams. Getting a reporter's job in 1966 was next to impossible.

There was one job opening for every 40 applicants. For me, it was incredible to land the biggest career change in my life. It was like an unexpected wealth, like a godsend. My stars were all in the right orbit.

My mother and father, bless their souls, had played a major role in my newspaper career, just by being good neighbors. When they decided to retire in Miami, Florida, in the early '60s, their neighbor's daughter, Elba Luisi, had taken an interest in my career. Elba, who worked in the advertising department of the *Miami Herald,* was aware that my parents wanted me to relocate to Florida. Although I had never met Elba, she volunteered to help. My parents also explained to her about my limited journalism experience, but that I was a former Army paratrooper, played high school sports, and, of course, spent time in New York City trying to become a prizefighter.

With almost non-existent credentials, I sent Elba my resume and she gave it to the *Miami Herald,* which rejected it. She did, however, say she had a good friend, Wilson McGee, the executive editor of the *Orlando Sentinel,* and that maybe he needed some help. McGee, who had worked with Elba at the *Miami Herald,* was hired by the Anderson family a couple of years earlier to run the Orlando newspaper. The Anderson family had just sold the paper to the *Chicago Tribune.* The *Tribune* decided to increase its staff because of a pending newspaper circulation war with the Gannett chain. Al Neuharth would be Gannett's general in Brevard County's battlefield, 40 miles from Orlando. Neuharth went on to publish *USA Today.*

My mother never lived to see me relocate to Florida. She died in Miami just before I moved to Florida. It was a devastating time for me and our family. She was the architect of our lives, made everything stable for us. We all loved her very much. I think of her often and miss her dearly. My father sold the Florida real estate, moved back to New York and lived with my brother. Only my sister, Kate, would remain in Florida.

Looking out the port window of a United Airlines commercial jet heading for Orlando, I thought about the "know your friends" phrase and I let out a chuckle on the plane. A few passengers looked over, and one said, "Are you all right?"

"I am just great," I answered.

I wanted to jot down a note to all of my friends, thanking them for choosing another barber.

Chapter 8
Would Orlando Kick
Off My Dream?

This one step—choosing a goal and sticking to it—
changes everything.
—Scott Reed

The United Airline commercial jet began its descent at the Orlando Airport in near perfect weather on a day in July 1966. Out the plane window I caught a view of the unspoiled landscape below me, an intense panorama of thick greenery. What a welcome to a new life for me and my family—if I got the job.

As the plane touched down on the runway, I glanced at my watch. Five o'clock in the afternoon—what a great time to be arriving, when the sun had the right slant to highlight the beautiful and restful surroundings that I hoped would become my new home.

As the plane moved toward the gate, the "what if's" hit. Tomorrow could be one of the most important days of my life.

Walking toward luggage pickup, my steps were lively while my mind sang, "Just One More Chance." How many years, playing at being a prizefighter, barber, and other odd endeavors, had I dreamed that with half a chance I could be a first-rate news reporter? Following plenty of rejections and ridicule, less than twenty-four hours from now I would have that chance—an interview for a reporter's job with the *Orlando Sentinel* newspaper.

Thinking about working for one of the largest newspapers in the state of Florida sent me into orbit. If the interview goes well, maybe the job was mine. My heart kept pace with my rapid footsteps. I grabbed my luggage, hurried to the curb, and waved down a cab to take me to the Holiday Inn.

"First time in Orlando?" the cab driver asked, looking me over through his cab mirror.

"First time in Florida," I said. "Orlando has a feeling I like."

"It's quiet here, sometimes too quiet. Many people like it that way. If you're looking for a drink on Sunday, forget it. This part of Orange County is dry on Sunday." And he repeated, "But some people like it that way."

"I can use a little of that quiet."

"Keep in mind if you are looking for action, it's over in Brevard County. Cocoa Beach. It's called the Platinum Coast, near the Kennedy Space Center. Bars open late seven days a week. Lots of action."

I chuckled inwardly at his thinly veiled tries to hustle me for a big fare.

He pulled in front of the hotel, took out of one of his cards. "If you ever want to go to Cocoa Beach, call me. My fare is reasonable."

Thanking him, I forked over a twenty-dollar bill like one of the nouveau rich. "Keep the change."

"Thanks, and hang onto my card."

I checked into the hotel, unpacked, and then called New York to let my family know I had arrived. Then, for dinner, I had a broiled bluefish and iced coffee. A walk might get my feet on the ground. My head was in the clouds. I might be dreaming instead of really, really being here. Orlando's cleanness and quietness set me picturing once again my living and working in this section of Florida. The little shops and streets looked quaint and orderly. The very atmosphere of Orlando for me was a call to action.

Early evening and time for a bit of cooling off, but the air retained the heat and humidity. Not many breezes stirred the green foliage. If that turned out to be Orlando's only drawback, though, I could tolerate that. Palm trees moved with only a gentle sway. They looked so straight and almost still. The center of the state, especially in July, seldom gets the refreshing breeze that Florida's coast enjoys, or so I've been told. Hearing thunder in the distance, I headed back to my hotel before the rain came. I breathed contentment when later a heavy shower added to my feeling of familiarity.

The next morning, I dressed in a dark navy suit; a little heavy for this heat, but the only one I packed. I managed to smile naively. It was only eight o'clock, a full hour before my appointment. The sun was bright and I already felt sweat trickling down my back.

Ambling along Orange Avenue, I was in no rush to end the short walk from the hotel to the *Orlando Sentinel*. A sense of confidence overwhelmed me. Who know where it came from? With an unexplainable sureness, I knew I finally would be a newsman. What if I was wrong?

I circled the building until the time for the appointment with the editor, Wilson McGee. On the dot, feeling the rush of confidence return, I entered the building. A few minutes later, his secretary escorted me into his office that looked more like a living room than an office. A beautiful purple wallpaper covered the walls. Seated in a deep, comfortable chair behind the desk sat a slender man with graying hair combed straight back. My heart pounded a little harder. He wore a white shirt and a red tie. Wilson McGee looked me over from his clear, blue eyes. I was grateful to see he wore no coat.

"So nice to meet you, Carl Veno." He came from behind the desk to shake my hand. "And take the jacket off. You will find most men in Florida walk around without a suit jacket."

"Thank you." The gesture of removing my coat raised my self-confidence even more. It gave me a sense of "I'm here to stay."

Back at his desk, he looked at my resume. "I see you have almost no experience as a writer, so what makes you think I should hire you to work for the Orlando Sentinel?" His steely but kind eyes challenged me to answer a question I knew he'd ask.

"A lot of knowledge about life, for one thing, Mr. McGee. I'm competitive about everything I do. I know sports, and my education is broad enough to be an asset to the newspaper."

I paused to straighten my shoulders and eye him straight on. "I am asking for a chance to prove myself. You won't be sorry. What I lack in writing experience, I'll make up in energy."

"I like your confidence and courage, Carl, but I need more than that. I need good reporters who dig deep and come up with the right stories and the supporting facts. I've also had training in law, and I know the importance of truth and fact." he said.

"I'm not looking for a dreamy fiction reporter. I want someone who will get the story straight. Our copy editors will edit your writing, and if it's bad, you'll be told in no uncertain terms. If your facts are wrong, no one can help you, and you've landed the newspaper in deep water."

"I understand." In spite of the air conditioning, sweat beaded on my forehead. And it wasn't altogether from the heat.

"If we employ you, it will be on a 90 day probationary period. At the end of that period, I will let you know if you are good enough to work for this fine newspaper. If not—" His penetrating gaze finished the sentence.

"I'll work hard," I said. "You won't be sorry if you hire me." I hoped *my* eyes conveyed my own determination.

"You're at least going to have a chance." He stood and leaned forward across his desk.

"All I want is a chance," I told him.

A battery of tests awaited me, and a background check, of course.

"Unless you run into serious trouble with a background check and the tests, you're hired. If all goes well, I will notify personnel and the Cocoa Beach Bureau Chief that a new reporter will be there in two weeks." He shook my hand. "I like your confidence. Don't lose that quality. In this business, the public and your newspaper will test it quite often. Get your facts, find the truth, and you'll do fine."

I put my jacket across my arm. "I'll do my best, Mr. Wilson."

His eyes locked on me. "Do better than your best."

I smiled and felt my self-assurance soaring.

"Oh, one more thing. Say hello to Elba. We worked together at the *Miami Herald*. She's one bright woman."

"I'll do that, and she is quite a gal." In the personnel department,

I went though a battery of tests and my score was good. That left only the background check, which I knew would be fine.

When I stopped by the office my last day in Orlando, I met Mrs. Anderson, the wife of the former owner of the newspaper. Surprised to see her doing secretarial work, I guessed she wanted to keep busy.

"You're Carl Veno? I understand you'll probably be going to Cocoa Beach."

"Yes, and I'm delighted."

"It's a lively area and the hotbed of a newspaper war."

"I heard that from Mr. McGee."

"Have no fear. When the bodies are cleared out, we'll be in the winner's circle." My answer was a smile. What a vivacious lady with a twinkle in her eye.

"We'll drive Gannett right out of Brevard County. They came in and started a new rag right in our backyard."

I nodded my head. "Hope I'll be there to do my part."

Everyone at the newspaper talked about the newspaper war in Brevard County. Two big newspaper giants were battling for circulation in one of the fastest growing counties in the United States. Soon the Orlando newspaper would have even more to protect.

Walt Disney decided to build a colossal playground in central Florida a few miles from Orlando called Walt Disney World. It would create one of the one of the riches advertising markets in the country. Orlando could go from a quaint, oversized hamlet to an overcrowded metropolitan area overnight. I could see traffic jams rivaling New York City. Motels would pop up everywhere. Nothing would be the same again.

If the Orlando Sentinel lost the battle in Brevard County, it could lose the war in Orlando. The survival of the newspaper was at stake.

What a thrill to think I could be at the scene of the battle and a part of it. My interviews finished, I flew back to New York in a happy, if nervous, haze to await the final phone call. Two days later, I could breathe again. I was officially a newspaper reporter.

When the news surfaced, most of my friends were happy, some

were skeptical, and a few spoke with a deep-seated envy.

However, none challenged my courage.

"He is a street fighter with big balls," said one of my friends.

"I can believe it," said another.

"He knows nothing about writing. His background is far from scholar status. Is he the same guy who was a lousy barber, a boxer, a milkman, a railroad worker, a bakery driver, a factory worker, and a pizza restaurant owner and ran a poker game?" said another critic.

Some would have to wait to see if I could make it.

This time I sang aloud: "Florida, Here I Come" to the tune of "California, Here I Come."

Ten days later, I landed once again in Florida to look for a place to live and start to work.

I'd never have to impersonate a barber again.

Chapter 9
Becoming a Man of Value

*None of us knows what the next change is going to
be, what unexpected opportunity is just around the
corner, waiting a few months or a few years to
change all the tenor of our lives.*
—Kathleen Norris, *Hands Full of Living*

The next change in my life started my career as a newspaper reporter. I pinched myself every minute or so to be sure I wasn't dreaming. No farewell party shot me out of my hometown, no going away gifts. I sold the barbershop, cleaned up my personal business, and I was gone. My wife and daughter stayed behind until I could find a place to live.

Two days of sleepless driving in a used 1960 Buick faced me. I thought about a myriad of things as the scenery whizzed by.

As I pulled into the outskirts of Orlando, I made a vow to follow Mahatma Gandhi's advice: "You must be the change you wish to see in the world."

First, I needed to sign some insurance papers at the main office and then report to the Cocoa News Bureau.

My car was heating up and required a few repairs, which meant I would have to leave it in Orlando for a day. I needed to get to Cocoa, about 40 miles from Orlando. The personnel manager arranged a ride for me. The reporter, Jay Sharbutt, would be waiting for me in the parking lot. The name sound familiar, but I couldn't place it.

I grabbed my luggage and walked out to the parking lot to meet Jay, who was the entertainment columnist for the *Sentinel* in Brevard County. He was a typical '60s hippie, twenty-something, longish hair, and a guitar strung over his shoulder. He drove a small foreign convertible.

"Put your things in the back and hop in," he said.

Then I jumped in front with him and we headed for the Cocoa news office.

Pleasant enough, we talked. Jay was a little reserved, but polite.

Driving down the highway, it finally hit me where I heard his name. His father was Del Sharbutt, a famous radio announcer. He did not want to talk about his father, and I didn't carry it any further.

"I understand you are going to be starting in sports," he said.

"Yes, I'm going to enjoy it immensely. Love sports."

Jay did not seem like the sports type, but I didn't care. I was trying to find something to talk about.

I finally dragged out of him that he was from New York City. At that moment I thought we did have something in common. We were both New Yorkers, but after some small talk, we had nothing more to say. It was difficult to strike up any lasting conversation. We had very little in common and the chemistry wasn't there.

At last, I struck a chord with the Vietnam War. I told him about being an Army paratrooper. Jay brightened up. Without hesitation, he told he wanted to be a war correspondent in Vietnam. That really surprised me. He didn't say why. He just wanted to be a war correspondent. Maybe he liked the sound of the title, or the romantic adventure of war.

"Sounds interesting. I hope you land it," I said.

With that, we were approaching the Cocoa Beach News Bureau and our conversation ended.

Although Jay and I worked in the same office together, we had a distant relationship. He was a fair columnist, covering the Cocoa Beach nightclub scene, but his ambitions were elsewhere.

Jay did get his wish and traveled to Vietnam as a war correspondent, working for a wire service. I never read any of his war stories, but he came back and got a big job with Associated Press as a national entertainment writer. His column appeared in most of the daily newspapers around the country. I found out later he had a serious heart condition and died in his forties.

That day, Jay pulled up to the front of the stucco building with almost no windows that housed the Cocoa Beach newspaper offices in the middle of town. I guess it was because of stormy weather and perhaps for privacy. "Thanks for the lift." I reached in the back seat to get my luggage.

He smiled. "My pleasure. See you around." He pulled away to park his car.

I brushed my suit, straightened my tie, picked up my suitcase and headed for the office door. *It was my first day on the job.*

The secretary knew who I was right away. "Welcome to Brevard County," she said. "I'm Mary. Mr. McBride will be out in a moment."

I sat down in a reception chair to wait. The air conditioning felt refreshing. The Cocoa news office was a cream color. I looked through the office window and saw some 20 reporters pounding away on typewriters. It was a few years before the computer age, of course, and the clamorous tapping rang through the lobby. I noticed a few reporters at their desks, waving their hands and probably chatting about some important story.

Waiting on the outside lasted only a few minutes. Blandon McBride, the editor of the Brevard County Bureau, walked out to greet me. He was in charge of all news operations in Brevard County, which included the Kennedy Space Center. He had a tough job, trying to stop the new kid on the block, *Brevard Today*, from gobbling up the good news stories in Brevard County.

"Carl, come on back to my office." A man in his early fifties, McBride was a big-built Southerner with a pleasant voice.

I followed the editor through the newsroom. A few reporters looked up and smiled, others were unaware and kept pounding away on their typewriters.

"I'll call in Jack Snyder, the assistant editor." Snyder, a smaller, partly balding man smiled and appeared a little shy.

"Welcome to Brevard, Carl."

It didn't take me long to find out that Jack was an excellent writer and editor. He was not ambitious, but was one of the most talented newspaper people I have ever met. Jack and I became good friends. We went to the racetrack in Orlando a few times and got drunk. I even attended his wedding reception. Jack was a true friend. He eventually took over McBride's job as editor.

"You're going in the sports department to work with Sports Editor Ralph Muller," McBride said. "Sports are important. Parents buy the paper so they can see their kids' names and pictures in it. I'll introduce you to Ralph in a few minutes."

It wasn't much of a pep talk, but I thought it was just his style. McBride asked me where I was from and what I knew about news and sports. He nodded his head, but seemed to have his mind elsewhere. McBride was a man who lacked the drive and energy that I have seen in a great leader. My gut feeling about him would prove right.

In a few months he would be fired.

He stressed how important it was to beat a fast-growing *Florida Today*, the Gannett newspaper that went from zero to 40,000 circulation in a few years. The *Orlando Sentinel's* newspaper, the *Brevard County Sentinel*, was losing circulation by the thousands. We never got the real numbers, but they were bad. Everybody had to work extra hard or else. It was a real war.

I walked out of McBride's office and there was Ralph Muller to meet me. He was a big guy from Green Bay, Wisconsin. He looked like a football linebacker. A former president of a minor league baseball team somewhere in Wisconsin, Ralph knew lot about sports and sports figures. He was a good sports writer and a nice, patient gentleman. This gentle giant was just the kind of editor I needed. He was full of enthusiasm, a virtue that was not widespread at the newspaper.

"Carl, I am so glad to meet you, and boy do we need help here. *Today* is handing us our heads. I'll tell you more about it later."

He invited me to dinner so we could talk about what my duties would be.

"Why don't you leave now so you can settle in a little," he said. "You can probably get a room for a couple of weeks at the Ko Ko Motel on the beach until you find something else. The motel also has a good a restaurant, and it's not far from the office."

Before I left, Ralph showed me around the newsroom, introduced me to the reporters, issued me my press credentials and assigned me a desk.

He shook my hand again. "I'll see you tonight about six o'clock for dinner at the Ko Ko. I'm sure you're going to work out just fine," he said. "Wait out front and I'll get you a ride to the hotel."

I thanked him, walked out, and hopped into the van that would take me to the hotel. As we drove over the causeway to Merritt Island and finally to Cocoa Beach, I caught a glance of the Kennedy Space Center. My heart rate doubled in that instant.

How exciting to be here with a front row seat to witness man's journey into space, the challenges that lay ahead, and the unexpected tragedies.

Chapter 10
Life at Cocoa Beach

It was the best of times, it was the worst of times.
  —Charles Dickens, *A Tale of Two Cities*

Here I was in March 1966, feeling as if I had been a reporter all my life. Soon I found a lovely yellow stucco split-level home in Cocoa and the three of us were once again a family.

I worked mostly in sports, but it wasn't easy to ignore that two of the biggest newspaper chains in the country, the *Chicago Tribune* and the Gannett Group, were locked in a circulation battle. To top it off, Brevard County, Florida, home of the Kennedy Space Center, was the fastest growing county in the country.

It didn't take me long to grasp the total picture. Newspaper wars can be nasty and extremely costly. In the end, one would win the battle and the other would win the war. The newsroom in Cocoa, Florida, was loaded with talent but short on energy. I didn't see the "go the extra mile" effort I expected in a newspaper that was losing a circulation battle.

Management there showed a bit of confusion. The *Chicago Tribune,* new owner of the *Orlando Sentinel,* looked for answers without finding any. As a tough competitor, I was disappointed to see such a defeatist attitude in the newsroom. Everyone I talked to was jumping ship looking for another job.

The Orlando newspaper had given me a wonderful job opportunity and I intended to show them how grateful I was by working hard. Most of our reporters had a different attitude. They moaned daily about how the new *Florida Today* newspaper was so superior to the *Orlando Sentinel.* Some were trying to switch sides. The *Sentinel* had lost some 30,000 subscribers in a matter of months and you could feel panic in the air.

The Gannett chain's publisher, Al Neuharth, the genius behind the newspaper, had almost a God-like image. Everyone talked about him. He put *Florida Today* together, and it became the fastest growing newspaper in Florida. The layout was designed to make reading easier with artfully designed display ads, great pictures, and attractive color. The new kid on the block hired good and loyal employees.

I heard Neuharth had an ego beyond the stars. Apparently he was not "Mr. Personality." His persona radiated that of a winner, however, and that was all that mattered. However, Neuharth deserves all the credit he received. He also is the founder of *USA Today*, the very successful daily national newspaper. He never lets the world forget. Neuharth makes sure that the title, *Founder,* is on all his columns.

Thanks to Sports Editor Ralph Mueller, I became a better sportswriter and even started writing a few news stories. Although many employees at Cocoa thought that *Florida Today* was going to blow the *Sentinel* out of Brevard County, Ralph and I never gave up hope. I worked hard, seven days a week. I covered every conceivable sport—boxing, Little League games and the Houston Astros farm baseball team. There was a time when we were told to take a picture of every Little Leaguer in the county to attract readers. We did. I even interviewed and took pictures of Mohammed Ali for a local story.

I had a lot of fun in sports. Two major league baseball players I enjoyed very much were Dean Chance and Bo Belinsky. Mueller knew them. Playboy Belinsky pitched for the Los Angeles Angels. He was as well-known for his dates with Hollywood starlets as for his pitching. Chance was a 20-game winner for the Angels and a Cy Young Award recipient. We had dinner and got half-drunk in one of the nightclubs in Cocoa Beach. They were two great ballplayers. Bo really had a way with women. They just loved him. I was sorry to read that he died in 2002.

I branched out from sports to write stories that included a day in a black county prison, which I found fascinating. Segregation was still raging in the South. I don't recall seeing any black reporters in either in *Orlando Sentinel* or *Florida Today,* not then. No one questioned it, even though Martin Luther King Jr. was traveling back and forth in Central Florida, campaigning for civil rights.

Our sports department mistakenly ran a picture of a black high football star instead of the headlined white player. We were flooded with calls. One irate caller said, "You know, it's a crime to call a white man black." None of us went to jail.

I was later assigned to the Titusville news office about 15 miles from Cocoa. I covered sports and whatever news was available. Chip Miller was the Bureau Chief in Titusville. I thought he was a great writer and editor. He had worked for the Associated Press in Montgomery, Alabama, and covered some of the civil rights stories in the early '60s.

We became very close friends, a relationship that would become more and more meaningful. He was a quiet, Southern gentleman with a lot of newspaper savvy. Miller changed my life when he convinced me to work for him at the *Yonkers Herald Statesman*, in Yonkers, New York, a Gannett newspaper.

In 1967, I thought the *Tribune* management made a mistake and the Gannett chain did not take advantage of it. The *Tribune* cut back the Brevard County operation by 50 percent. It was a sign of defeat. Management was convinced that moving back to Orlando to protect its home base was best.

My employer almost abandoned Brevard County, which left the road to Orlando wide open for Gannett to move in. Some thought the strategy made Orlando vulnerable. Surrender Brevard today and lose Orlando tomorrow. The *Tribune,* not known for its generous pay scale, decided to save money by keeping a small news team in Brevard County to cover the space program and the local news. *Florida Today* was declared the champion.

Cocoa Editor Blandon McBride was removed and a number of

reporters were laid off. As one of the youngest reporters who didn't have any seniority, I thought I would be heading back to Olean, but my name never appeared on a pink slip. Mueller went to work in Orlando for a while and then quit to go to a Johnsonville newspaper.

The *Tribune* began raiding executives from Gannett. They hired Martin Greco, a circulation manager, which proved to be a lucky break for me. Greco interviewed me and found out I was a New Yorker and we hit it off. He talked about his work at the famous *Brooklyn Eagle*, a small but feisty paper in New York. Greco was a nice guy, no real heavyweight, but better than the former editor, McBride.

I was transferred to Orlando to work on the state copy desk. It was a promotion for me. I continued to live in Cocoa and drove to Orlando every day.

Meanwhile, the raiding of newsmen continued and this time it was Gannett stealing Orlando people. They landed Chip Miller*, who took an editor's job in Yonkers, New York. When I heard about it, I was puzzled. Here was a Southerner who had never lived in the North, and he had decided to take a job in Yonkers. I did not think it was a good move for him, but I wished him luck.

It was a tough time for the *Orlando Sentinel. Florida Today* had them on the ropes and was about to knock them out of a rich advertising market.

While the newspaper battle was going on, Walt Disney decided to put Walt Disney World right in the middle of central Florida. I thought that if Gannett moved into Orlando and put on the show they did in Brevard County, then it could walk away with the advertising market there, too. In my view, the *Sentinel* was ripe for the taking. They were still reeling from the beating they took in Brevard County and did not have much time to reorganize. Chaotic times continued in Orlando.

Hardly a day went by that someone wasn't fired or quit. Wilson McGee, the editor who hired me, retired. The publisher, Bill Colomos, was fired. Everything seemed to be in disarray on Orange Avenue in Orlando.

Why the Gannett chain did not try to take over Orlando still remains a mystery to me. Whatever kept them out of Orlando proved a bonanza for the *Orlando Sentinel*.

They lost the battle in Brevard County, but won the war in central Florida.

The *Orlando Sentinel* now is the top newspaper in central Florida. *Florida Today* still controls the circulation in Brevard County with about 116,000 Sunday subscribers.

The *Sentinel* still has a number of loyal readers in Brevard County, but nowhere near the number Gannett maintains.

In retrospect, if Gannett had launched its newspaper in Orlando with a strong circulation push, it might have succeeded knocking off the number one newspaper in Orlando.

In a twist of events, the newspaper war would change my fate and direction of my life again.

Now that the dust of the newspaper war had settled, our focus changed to space.

Chapter 11
The Apollo Deaths

Death and sorrow will be the companions of our journey ...
—Winston Churchill

The split-level home where I lived in on Sunrise Street overlooked the blue, clear waters of the Indian River and provided a spectacular view of the Kennedy Space Center satellites streaming into the heavens. The Space Center, a few miles in the distance, frequently displayed a breathtaking panorama of spacecrafts blazing into orbit.

Incredible space journeys were planned in 1967. NASA looked to a moon voyage, possible trips to Mars, and perhaps a grand tour of the galaxy. Nothing appeared beyond our reach in the Space Age. However, with success comes a price.

The danger of failure and loss of life was always present. You could feel the intensity on every liftoff and on every exercise. Only after a completed mission is there a long sigh of relief. In 1967, the US space program hailed a six-year impeccable safety record, putting 19 Americans in space in six years without a serious injury. It was a remarkable record for a dangerous business.

Vigilance never rests at the Cape, even with ground space training, considered safer than space flight. In spite of the perpetual safeguards, something went horribly wrong on January 27, 1967.

Early that Friday morning, I enjoyed a hearty breakfast, read the newspaper, and prepared for a newsroom meeting in Cocoa. It would be a long day for me since I had to cover an event that night. My father, who was visiting from New York, puttered in the outside flower garden. He plucked large grapefruits, filling a small basket nearby.

Earlier in the week, Astronaut Virgil "Gus" Grissom yanked a ripe yellow lemon from his front yard tree to take to work. He attached it to the problem-plagued training simulator, a joke he played on the work crew. The simulator had nagging problems and setbacks that never seemed to end.

Before going to work, I grabbed a newly-purchased camera on my desk and took a few quick snapshots of my two-year-old daughter Anne. The family was getting ready to do the weekend shopping at Publix Market. It appeared to be a normal, uneventful day.

I invited my father to go with me while I worked on a story outside the office in central Brevard County. Later, a fellow reporter, somber-faced with tears in his eyes, walked up to us. "You probably haven't heard."

Without warning, a ground procedure had quickly turned into an inferno death storm. Devastating!

A ground procedure? My father and I stood in shock as we listened to the story. We had little to say.

Across the Indian River at Cape Kennedy's Launch Complex 34, command module 102 sat atop a Saturn IB. The astronauts were getting ready for the launch simulation, an important step in determining if the spacecraft would be ready to fly in February. The ground test was part of the first manned Apollo flight, another step closer to the moon.

The three space-suited astronauts, Virgil Grissom, Edward White, and Roger Chafee, slid into the spacecraft couches, checking systems. The crew sealed the hatch tight and locked it. The astronauts began purging all the gases in the cabin except oxygen, a regular procedure. That day, the trial presented minor communication problems. Finding the problem and fixing it consumed time. Long delays and rechecking are common and tedious, but necessary. Other systems seemed to be operating normally, the crew reported.

Grissom, who was chosen with the first group of astronauts in

1959, was named commander of the first Apollo flight. Early that evening, the three astronauts were still sealed in the capsule.

The earth stood still in the control room when the cry blasted over the radio circuit. "There's a fire in here!"

A sheet of flame flashed from the spacecraft, followed by an explosion. Rescue teams rushed to the smoked-filled area. The three astronauts were trapped inside the pure oxygen-filled capsule.

"Blow the hatch, why don't they blow the hatch?" cried one of the workers.

Later investigation showed that the hatch could not be opened explosively, making it impossible for the crew to escape. Trapped inside a sealed capsule, survival slipped away with each precious second. It would take five and one half minutes to pry open spacecraft hatches.

According to a NASA report, the doctors and the rescue team reached the three astronauts fifteen minutes later, but it was too late. They were burned badly and had died from inhaling toxic gases.

Everyone was in shock. President Johnson and the nation mourned.

What went wrong?

A review board reported that a sealed cabin pressurized with an oxygen atmosphere was one condition that led to the disaster and inadequate provision for the crew to escape was another. The cause of the fire itself was unclear. A final word pointed to an electrical spark. The board called for major design and safety overhauling.

Finger pointing became the game. Senator Walter Mondale raised questions of negligence on the part of NASA management and the prime contractor, North American.

Nonmetallic and flammable materials including foam were investigated. Foam was something we would hear about again in the Space Shuttle Columbia disaster of January 2003.

Newspaper editorials raised more questions. More investigations were conducted. Fired NASA employees leaked stories to the press about sloppy and incompetent work. It was a heartbreaking time at the Space Center.

Working near the space center, following the events, getting to know the workers and astronauts was like belonging to a big family. The loss of one of the members is soul- wrenching.

The deaths shocked everyone, especially when they happened during a ground test. Forcefully, we were reminded how dangerous the space program can be.

In a press interview weeks before, Grissom made a strong statement. "We are in a risky business, and if anything happens to us, it must not delay the program. The conquest of space is worth the risk of life."

Not everyone agreed with him. The calls to suspend the space program increased. "Too risky and too expensive," voiced analysts and politicians. The Apollo 204 fire was a setback for the space program, but not the end. President Johnson paid tribute to the astronauts, and then pushed for the program to go on. The review board would find deficiencies but not enough to scrub the space program.

"Fix it, start again," was the philosophy.

Come to think of it, that phrase sums up my newspaper life. "Fix it, start again."

As I watched the Space Shuttle Columbia tragedy in which seven astronauts perished, in 2003, I was reminded of the fateful day, January 27, 1967.

The grief for our departed space heroes did not stop us from going forward.

Two years after the 1967 tragedy, on July 21, 1969, Apollo 11 Model *Eagle* landed on the moon. Astronauts Neil Armstrong, Michael Collins, and Edwin Aldrin completed the long-awaited mission.

Carried to the moon were two large American flags. The country glowed with patriotic pride.

Even with the setback of the tragedies of the Apollo program, I knew back in January 1967, we would achieve the goal of reaching the moon and the stars.

And I know it's only the beginning. What I am never prepared for is the price we must pay.

Chapter 12
Trading Oranges for
the Big Apple

Without change, something sleeps inside us,
and seldom awakens. The sleeper must awaken.
—Frank Herbert

The phone call caught me at my copy desk in Orlando on a day in July—much like the day I had first landed in Florida—hot, humid, and happy. Waiting for more news copy to arrive, I debated buying a house in Orlando because the thirty-mile commute from Cocoa Beach twice a day had lost its charm.

Should I wait, though, for the feature writer's job back in Brevard County? Although I'd been promised the position, I had no idea how soon it would materialize. It might be a good investment to go ahead and get a house here because news was popping at the *Sentinel* that would send property values soaring.

Walt Disney's plan to build Walt Disney World in central Florida set off a buzz of excitement that spread through the entire area. The newspaper had an advertising gold mine in its grasp. A small, quiet, scenic area would explode into a bustling metropolis. Strategy on how to protect the bonanza concerned management.

The *Sentinel* lost an enormous amount of circulation in Brevard County to the Gannett newspaper. The *Chicago Tribune*-owned newspaper in Cocoa Beach worried about a battle in its backyard. No one could be certain what Gannett planned for *Florida Today*, a beautifully designed newspaper that the readers loved. I think it would have sold big time in Orlando.

Gannett had a popular newspaper to move in central Florida, but for unknown reasons, it lost a golden opportunity to take over Orlando. The newspaper war in Brevard County would not spill over into Orlando. The *Orlando Sentinel* won the Orlando battle by default.

I could turn a tidy profit by buying a house in Orlando and maybe invest in land. After all, I had a view of possibilities long before the investors decided to rush down and buy everything. Millions of dollars would be made and I stood on the ground floor—at the right place and the right time. A once-in-a-lifetime opportunity stared me in the face. With my knowledge of the area, I had the opportunity to make the fortune I'd waited for all my life.

But I wasn't going to leave journalism for real estate. I had worked too hard to become a newspaperman. If I had to do it over again, I would do the same thing. When you find something you enjoy, money isn't everything.

I think I made my firm decision at about the moment that unexpected phone call came. Gannett was still raiding reporters from the *Sentinel*. Our Orlando paper played the same game with Gannett. In July 1967, Chip Miller, the former *Orlando Sentinel* Bureau Chief, called me from Yonkers, New York. I was surprised to hear from him since he switched to the Gannett chain. He was now City Editor at the *Yonkers Herald Statesman*.

"How would you like to work in Yonkers?" he said.

"What the hell would I do in Yonkers?"

Since I was from New York, he thought I might be interested coming back to work near New York City.

"The newspaper needs a strong leader. Bob Martin*, the Managing Editor, wanted to know if you were interested," Chip said. "I also talked to the top man, Editor Barney Waters, who worked for the *Miami News* and he would be in favor of it."

"A good thing I'm sitting down," I said. It wasn't easy to hide my excitement at the idea of going close to home, no matter how much I loved Florida. "Otherwise I would have fallen down."

"You would work on the news copy desk and maybe get one of the chain newspapers in Westchester County. Gannett bought several newspapers in the county and shifted the leadership around."

"And?" I said.

"You would also help with the *Mount Vernon Argus*, a small newspaper in Mount Vernon. That newspaper might be up for grabs."

"Let me talk it over with my family, and I'll get back to you in a few days," I said, not believing what I'd heard and how my heart was somersaulting.

It was a huge and tough decision to make. I lived in a beautiful place, my job was secure, and Walt Disney World was coming. I could only go one way: up. I had lived in the New York City area. It's expensive and it's hard to find a place to live.

In Orlando I had even been promised a feature writer's job that would spring me loose from the copy desk. Central Florida was a great place to raise a family. Contentment had become a habit. So what is there to think about? I still couldn't convince myself that I wanted to turn down the lure of the New York offer.

I needed more time to think. A talk with my family left the decision on my shoulders. I took a day off work, drove out to Cocoa Beach and walked a few miles alone along the ocean. If it had been any place other than New York, I would not hesitate a second to turn the offer down. Chip knew my love for the New York area, and I wanted to see what was waiting for me once again in New York. I did have friends there and I would be closer to my relatives.

After hours and hours of soul searching, I decided to take the job. It would be a big gamble, but I had run my life taking high risks and living on the edge. So far it had worked out.

I called Chip three days later. "I'll take it."

"I didn't think you were going to take the job." He sounded thrilled, but no more so than I, despite my mixed feelings. "Can you be at work in three weeks?"

"Give me a month and I'll be there."

"Okay, I'll see you on August 17th."

We agreed on the pay, traveling expense, and job position. The hardest part was giving notice of my departure to the *Orlando Sentinel*.

I walked into the office of Robert J. Howard, my managing editor. His forehead furrowed into wrinkles. "This is quite a shock," he said. "I thought you were happy here. And we even promised you that feature's writer job back in Brevard."

"That made my decision even harder. You can't imagine how I appreciate the *Sentinel* giving me a chance as a reporter—the break of my life. Had it been anyplace but New York, no way I'd be leaving."

He smiled. "You're going where?"

"Yonkers," I said.

"You're trading Disney for the racetrack?"

"No, oranges for the Big Apple," I answered.

We both laughed and the atmosphere relaxed.

"You must be the only person leaving central Florida. Disney is coming south and you are going north. Don't forget us," he said.

"Never happen."

We shook hands. Then he put his hand on my shoulder. "Take care and good luck."

I smiled all the way back to Cocoa Beach.

Here I go again.

Chapter 13
Leaving Florida with Memories

We do not know the true value of our moments
Until they have undergone the test of memory.
—George Duhamel, *The Heart's Domain*

Changes don't always start out on a melodious note. Forget thinking straight on the backbreaking train ride from Orlando to the new Pennsylvania Station in New York City. The three of us spent two days of discomfort, broken only by moments of sheer misery, aboard the Silver Meteor.

Trying to get comfortable on the hard, vinyl seats could be compared to a ride on a wild Texas bronco. My pregnant wife and two-year-old daughter, Anne, had an even rougher time than I did. The ride bumped along. It was anything but romantic. No love songs would be written about this trip.

Unavailable sleeping berths made the overnight 1,400-mile ride almost unbearable. Time dragged on and the body aches increased. New York City seemed light years away. Every whistle stop added to the boredom. I lost track of our location.

Pleasant dreams were impossible under these conditions. I wished I could be joyous over returning to New York and the copy editor's job that I would begin on Monday, August 21, 1967, at the *Yonkers Herald Statesman*. For now, I only wanted comfort. The sympathetic conductor allowed my wife two facing seats to ease the cramps in the swollen legs she painfully endured. Another jerk and jolt might have produced the miracle of birth. The train followed the same the route that the famous Orange Blossom Special did years ago. I wondered if those passengers underwent the same unpleasant experience.

The houses and green landscape that raced by the train window reflected flashes of memorable moments in Florida. If I couldn't think about the future, maybe I could remember the life I left behind. As we headed for Johnsonville and up the coast to New York City, my mind held onto the people and events that were certain to be in my memories forever. The high profile celebrities created an imprint, but the common folk touched my soul.

The phased-out Gibson High School in Brevard County with all black students overwhelmed me. I witnessed a new age coming to the south. Equal educational opportunities came in as segregation tumbled. However, the good news left some uncertain futures.

Ed Harris, the head football coach of the school, welcomed change with mixed emotions. Harris was delighted for the students, but I wondered where he'd wind up since his job had been sacrificed for progress. With the school closing, he would move on. Once in a while, I see him in my mind, but I never saw him again. I have no idea where he is now.

I remember of one of my favorite young fighters whom I covered on the boxing beat. Roscoe Bell, a tough, 160–pound middleweight bounced around heavyweights with ease. Bell had a bundle of athletic potential, but he had even better qualities outside the ring. Poverty-stricken most of his life, he lacked a formal education, had a speech impediment, couldn't read, and lived in the segregated south. Courage he didn't lack to confront his life's adversities. Bell combined his boxing skills with hard work.

The twenty-five-year-old black fighter tackled odd jobs and labored sixty or seventy hours a week to climb out of the bowels of misfortune. He confronted his handicaps with fortitude. Bell even bought a modest home for his family. He started school again to get a high school diploma.

The day his 13-month-old baby died of pneumonia, I felt a personal loss. This young man overcame many obstacles only to face more brick walls. After the funeral, he came into the gym to train. He did not mourn at home. Bell buried his tears and grief in his work. So special to me, I hope he's doing well.

Another significant person in my life, Johnny Esposito, managed Johnny's Hideaway, a nightclub on Cocoa Beach. John came to Florida with forty-three dollars in his pocket and parlayed those dollars into a comfortable living. I spent many an hour at the Hideaway, enjoying the lounge and soaking up good stories.

The Philadelphia native's nightclub consisted of a dance hall, dining room, and a cocktail lounge that all the celebrities patronized. Not bad for less than half-a-hundred dollar star. He introduced me to Chris and Angelo Dundee. Angelo was the famous trainer of Mohammed Ali. I later interviewed Ali.

Two of the most talented sportswriters I worked with were Van McKenzie and Sports Editor Ralph Mueller. I owe them so much for helping me improve my creative writing. I have no doubt that both went on great careers. I also took photos and worked with a fine photographer, Gene Blythe, the *Orlando Sentinel's* premier cameraman.

Although Editor Wilson McGee left the *Orlando Sentinel* before I quit, I owe my newspaper career to him. My writing skills fell short of those of the other applicants, but he hired me nonetheless. McGee looked for something in addition to the ability to write. He believed my toughness would be an asset to the newspaper war, and my writing ability would follow. The feisty editor didn't want a bookworm; he wanted an optimistic fighter to go after a story no matter what it entailed. His goal aimed at burying the competition. I attempted to accomplish his mission.

I never had a chance to say goodbye or thank him for the wonderful opportunity he put in my path. One day when I missed going in, he resigned, and disappeared. I heard he went back to the Miami area and retired. He wanted to be left alone. I still think of him often, and I always will.

Then there was the Apollo One tragedy in which the three astronauts were killed in a flash fire at Kennedy Space Center. I knew this would be a scar on my heart forever. Reliving that disastrous day and reviewing the life I left, I closed my eyes and found I could think about tomorrow. I dozed off into a light sleep and was awakened by the conductor's loud voice.

"New York City is only minutes away."

The Silver Meteor pulled into the new Pennsylvania Station at Felt Forum 33rd Street. The thoughts of yesterday during the previous hour had almost made me forget the weariness of the ride. My wife and daughter were laughing. We were here. What a relief.

Three years earlier, the beautiful old Pennsylvania Station vanished under a barrage of wrecking balls and bulldozers. A masterpiece of granite and steel, like the Orange Blossom Special, gave way to changing times.

We walked up steps into the Manhattan sunlight and hailed a taxi to take us to our apartment on Broadway, near Yonkers. Driving up Eighth Avenue, I passed the West 46th Street sign and remembered my youth and my dreams of becoming a professional boxer. I tried to find the apartment where I had lived twelve year earlier, but it was now gone, swept away and replaced. What had happened to the clerk who gave me "fatherly advice"? He would forever be in my mind a comical guy with a helpful heart.

In Lower Manhattan, three blocks north of the New York Stock Exchange, the World Trade Center was under construction and would eventually cover sixteen acres. It was an exciting time for the Big Apple and me. Sixteen miles away, the second stage of my newspaper career waited. The taxi sped along the West Side highway and across the Hudson River. I saw the Palisades as beautiful as twelve years ago.

I had returned. I always knew I would.

Chapter 14
First Day at the
Yonkers Herald Statesman

*Every man has his own destiny: the only imperative
is to follow it, no matter where it leads him.*
—Henry Miller, *The Wisdom of the Heart*

The gloom of the wet August Monday morning failed to dampen my enthusiasm. Fired up about my new job, through my eyes, the day looked bright and promising. I believed I was following my destiny.

I gulped down my second cup of coffee, gazed out the kitchen window of our Broadway apartment across from Central Park. The light rain gave a sparkling image to the green shrubbery and the trees. What a scenic forest with tranquil overtones in the middle of Manhattan.

Checking my watch again, I grabbed my leather briefcase and with brisk movements toward the door, I forgot to say goodbye. I spun around and came back to give my wife and daughter a kiss.

"Sorry—I'm a little nervous."

"You're forgiven, have a good day, and call me," she whispered from the lounge chair.

"I'll call around noon."

With a quick glance in the hallway mirror, I straightened my tie one more time, hurried to the elevator, went down to the first floor, and dashed across the street to the bus stop. I couldn't stop looking at my watch. *I can't be late my first day at the* Yonkers Herald Statesman.

The newspaper was part of a group Gannett purchased a few years earlier from the Macy family. Gannett made sweeping personnel changes in the Westchester County papers. I came in on the new wave. Difficult to believe that the previous year I had opposed Gannett in Florida.

I stood at the bus stop with half-asleep commuters leaving New York City to work in the suburbs. The transit bus stopped ahead of the commuters, so we made a dash to get aboard.

"Keep moving. I can't answer any questions," the grumpy bus driver barked before I had a chance to ask directions.

"I just want—"

"Listen, pal, is something wrong with your ears? Move."

As the bus jerked forward, I held onto the seats, wobbled to the rear of the bus and dropped down on my seat. I got my question answered from a polite woman passenger, who worked near the newspaper.

I allowed the rude bus driver to sour my upbeat mood. *Why is it the first guy I talk to this morning has to be an asshole?* Sitting there, the inevitable thoughts churned inside me again. *I might have made a mistake. Why did I leave the comforts of Florida for this shit? My destiny? Really! It wasn't fair to drag my pregnant wife 1400 miles to a small two-bedroom apartment in New York City.* I must have batted all this about a hundred times before.

I reassured myself once again that I made the right decision. *I am going to take this career wherever it leads me. There will be a purpose to it all. I am here for a reason.* My spirits lifted again. One stupid bus driver ticked me off, but he could never distract me from my journey.

The woman nudged me. "It's Larkin Plaza. You can see the newspaper from here."

"Thanks for your kind help," I said.

The bus stopped in front of the newspaper. I stood up, brushed off my suit, and more or less dived out the rear door. Stepping onto the pavement, I sighed with relief. I had arrived.

The sun peeked out from behind the clouds. A pleasant day after all, I concluded. Across the street from the newspaper, the New York Central Train Station loomed. A few yards from the train station was a little park that had no grass, but a litter of bottles, papers and leftover food wrappers. A light breeze carried a smell of incinerated metal.

The gray steel newspaper building towered against the background of the rusty Otis Elevator company, a factory with a world-famous name. Sitting at the other side of the *Herald Statesman*, the Casa D'Roma Restaurant would become my second home. On top of the hill a few yards from the restaurant, a historic building with the sign in the front gate read, "Washington slept here." He surely slept in a lot of places.

I pushed the bell on the newspaper street entrance. After a few minutes, a guard came to door. He checked my name and escorted me to Rose, the secretary on the second floor, at the entrance to the newsroom.

"Chip Miller is expecting me," I said.

"Hi, Carl," she answered in a pleasant voice. "You'll see and hear a lot of me while you're here."

Only seconds passed when Chip walked out to greet me with a broad smile. "You made it," he said, giving me a bear hug.

"I did, and I am ready to go."

The Associated Press ticker tape clicked away while we walked through the newsroom. All eyes were glued on me. Chip walked me by the desk reporters and into the editor's office to meet Bob Martin.

Martin, the managing editor, stood from behind his desk, gave me a hearty handshake, and sat down again. A cigar-smoking, tall and lanky Chicago transplant, he appeared relaxed and comfortable. He had my resume in front of him.

"Did Chip talk about what you would be doing?"

"He said I would be working at the copy desk and making up news pages," I answered.

"You'll be backing up David Hartley, our news editor." Martin said. "I'll introduce you to him and the rest of the newsroom. Today I want you to become familiar with everyone, and in the next few days we'll get you behind the desk."

Chip looked at his watch. "I got a ton of work, Carl, and you're in safe hands."

Hartley said, "We'll see you at lunch, Chip. Carl, the three of us will go next door for lunch. Is that okay with you?"

"I'd love it."

"I understand you were a boxer," Martin said.

"I did some boxing, but nothing to brag about. I thought I could make a living at it, but changed my mind."

"I hope you can use some of those aggressive skills to knock some heads around here," Martin said.

He caught me off guard. I did not expect that. I interpreted the statement to mean he wanted someone who ramrods the news team. He went over my duties in making up news pages and dealing out news stories to other copy editors to edit. I played a role in deciding where a story should go, inside or on the front page.

"We have a lot of people I'd like to get rid of, but we can talk about that later."

I remained silent for a moment. "I'll give it my all, Bob."

"Good. Let me introduce you to the editor and the rest of the people."

We walked into Editor Barney Waters' office. Barney was a middle-aged, potbellied Cuban native who worked for the *Miami News* before joining Gannett. A tough but good-hearted editor, he knew some big guns in the chain and landed the *Herald Statesman's* job as editor.

"I feel sure you're going to enjoy being here." We talked briefly and then Waters disappeared into his office.

Then in the newsroom, I met David Hartley, the news editor. "Don't worry about the job," he said. "You'll be fine." He talked very little about the job and more about family life. He was twenty-eight years old, married with two young boys. He loved to talk about Scotland, his Scottish heritage, and its traditions. He proved to be a hardworking editor and one of the most talented writers I had ever met.

"Don't forget—every payday, the newsroom people all go to lunch. And if you want to cash your check, I know a place on Nepperhan Avenue." David looked at me intently through steel-framed glasses and smoothed the few hairs on his balding head. Despite his small frame, he would never be overlooked in a crowd. Everyone liked David.

Each morning when I arrived at work about 6 a.m., David sat in the dark parking lot playing a bagpipe flute. After months of practice, he mastered the bagpipes and joined one of the local bands.

A different lifestyle appeared in New York, nothing like Florida, where alcohol helped calm the stressful. Some of the New Yorkers smoked pot. The late sixties and the Vietnam War saw a flow of heavy drug use. Later, when crack cocaine hit the streets, the devil surfaced with the cheap high drug. It changed the face of the urban landscapes.

There is a David in every company. He's there for life no matter how the company bounces him around. Win or lose, one job forever. I thought David lacked the kind of aggressiveness that gets one to the top. A talented writer and editor he was, but without a driving goal.

That first morning, I walked around the newsroom shaking hands until I met everyone. The next important step included meeting the production crew and the foreman. They held your fate in their hands. If they slowed down and the paper doesn't get out, you are dead in the water. If they disliked you, chances are your days are numbered from the start, no matter how bright and talented you are. They were tough, blue-collar workers, veterans and sports fans, my kind of people who added strength to my career.

Bill Bruce, the supervisor, played publisher and owner. A tall, flushed-face, nervous, chain-smoking guy, he could make your life miserable. His disabled son, Bill Jr., worked with the crew. Bill Jr., an ex-marine injured in an auto accident, loved to talk about sports, which gave us something in common. Bruce did, however, cause a few of the editors to get their walking papers.

The company had one editor named Jerry Bellune, a quiet Southerner and a boyhood friend of Chip Miller's. Jerry had a knack for creating great front pages, but it took time and work. Bill Sr. stayed on his case, and he was out the door. Jerry was simply one of the names Bill added to his hit list.

My friendship with the composing room guys provided an enormous plus for me. Kenny Schist, one of the compositors, and I became close friends. Kenny, a husky, hard worker and a tough drinker, believed he could get a top job by working for it. He found out differently. Kenny and I would drink together and talk about his goals. He ignored the fact that he had diabetes and at times drank too much.

The composing room had its share of ass kissers. Joe Garvey, who was Kenny's rival for the assistant supervisor's post, never failed to make the right points and it paid off.

Garvey would eventually get an executive production job with *USA Today*. Joe—tall and thin, with dark horn-rimmed glasses—had a smooth way about him. He had a great Irish wit and some talent to go with it. What he lacked in ability, he made up for in pushy ambition. Garvey's campaigning got his wife, Sally, a beautiful blonde and editor in the society department, an editor's job in Mount Vernon.

No matter where you work, ass kissing is difficult to compete with.

Talent and hard work wins prizes, but not the gold. I always ended up the bronze.

Even without the gold medal, I was certain I was following my path of destiny. *Where would my chosen road lead me?*

Chapter 15
Red and White Roses
for a Dead Lady

*... I've seen the devil of violence, and the devil of hot
desire, but, by all the stars! these were strong, lusty,
red-eyed devils that swayed and drove men ...*
—Joseph Conrad, *Heart of Darkness*

A few weeks after I went to work in Yonkers, a story came in that
attracted great readership. John Dipalo*, a tailor, and his lovely
blonde wife, Liz*, with startling green eyes, lived in Irvington, New
York. The twosome had an undisputed reputation of being the ideal
couple.

John and Liz appeared to love each other beyond words. They
were seen in Westchester restaurants holding hands and kissing in
public. What a romance. The lovebirds were the envy of every worn-
out, sputtering love affair.

John's flower bill overwhelmed the bragging florist. This
handsome Casanova with dark eyes and thinning black hair sent an
assortment of summer flowers and green plants daily to his wife. The
pleasant scent permeated their large, split-level home. Withered
flowers stacked up in the Dipalo backyard. Childhood sweethearts,
they had been married fifteen years. Everything seemed magical. His
tailoring business reached record numbers, and the fairy- tale
marriage looked like it would last forever.

On a warm, August day, the pleasant-mannered, well-dressed
tailor took a morning flight to Cleveland to attend an annual clothing

convention. John would be away for seven days. He called the florist and had an extra large bouquet of red and white roses delivered every day. With every lovely flower setting, the greeting card read the same, "Love Forever."

The Saturday night before he came home, the fragile little tailor received devastating news. His brother Sam called, sobbing into the phone, "Liz has been murdered."

The police found a ransacked bedroom with Liz's blood-soaked body on the floor. Someone had broken in the back door and stabbed Liz to death, leaving a scene of horror in the love nest. Forensic investigation ruled out rape. No valuables were taken. Police were puzzled. Stunned by the death of his beloved wife, John admitted himself to a Cleveland hospital. Sleeping pills kept the demons away that night.

After a tearful day in the hospital, John flew back to Irvington to mourn and to bury his wife. The police worked overtime on the much-publicized tragedy. In an amazingly short time, detectives came up with a prime suspect. His fingerprints were found on the murdered body and police recovered bloody gloves in his apartment. Charged with first-degree murder, ex-con Bill White* had plenty to tell the police.

John, still upset and tense, decided to leave town to grieve his lover's death.

Police grilled White into an admission. Why did he kill her? He finally confessed, stating Liz's husband, John, hired him for $50,000 to kill John's wife. White's signed confession shocked the community.

No one believed the low-life ex-con—that is until a one-million-dollar life insurance policy on Liz surfaced with John the beneficiary.

White, a petty thief and a confirmed drug user, had recently been released from Green Haven prison after a year for a burglary rap. John and White were grade school chums, but seldom fraternized. Now and then, though, they ran across each other at the diner and talked over coffee about school days.

John lived a normal life: a navy veteran, no criminal record, and no ghosts in his closets. A nose-to-the-grindstone businessman, he earned the respect of the community. If he ran for mayor, he would have won hands down. The dark side of John appeared in an obsession for expensive things—cars, jewelry, and a luxury boat for weekend cruises on the Hudson. One might ignore the desire for these playthings coming from such a hard-working tailor. He deserved the best.

White, on the other hand, was a career criminal, a social misfit, one who bounced in and out of jail most of his life. He found few believers. How can anyone believe a crook who woke up every morning planning to steal for his next high?

Only the ex-con and John's banker knew the tailor was heavily in debt. Mesmerized by the million-dollar insurance policy, he thought he found a way to live the good life debt-free. White said John talked about a million dollars and owing no taxes. What a life he could have with it! A sick, twisted way to end a life of a loving, innocent woman. John finally confessed. He said he really loved his wife but became blinded by the money. Did he love his wife? How do you kill the person you love? What is known is that he loved all things with a price tag. The love of John's life was money, not Liz.

Greed is a powerful, driving force. It starts wars, it kills, it deceives, and it lies. John hired White because he thought no one would believe the low-lifer. Any country lawyer could rip the ex-con's story to shreds. How many tailors have a million-dollar life insurance on their spouse? No amount of flowers could disguise that kind of insurance. The story got a lot of mileage and John got a lot of time.

With John safely locked away, things settled down a bit at the *Yonkers Herald Statesman*.

I took time to make a thorough search through the Bronx, Manhattan, and Westchester County. We found a beautiful garden apartment in Dobbs Ferry, New York, about 20 minutes from Yonkers. The charming hamlet, nestled in suburban Westchester

County, overlooked the Hudson River. It was situated a little distance from historic Irvington and Tarrytown, home of the Rockefeller estate. We had lucked out.

Unknown to me, Editor Bob Martin lived a few blocks away. Instead of renting, this tall, wiry newsman from Illinois purchased a charming, colonial four-bedroom home near a community park. We socialized little, but I did meet his attractive wife, Mary, and the family. The couple, in their mid-thirties, slipped into the high life of the community. Mary joined a church and clubs. Bob played golf and mingled with newspaper executives.

A far jump from the social scene, Chip Miller rented an apartment in a Yonkers high-rise, a questionable move. His apartment, only a few miles from the crime-ridden housing projects, kept Miller close to home. His wife, Kathy*, a tiny, attractive brunette, disliked the area and longed to return to her South Carolina birthplace. Chip and Kathy felt out of place and uncomfortable.

I detected the uneasiness after a few visits to their apartment. Life in Yonkers was not compatible to a country gentleman and his sweet Southern wife. Deeply religious, Chip and Kathy stayed much to themselves without social activities. A skilled city editor, Chip's unhappy social life never affected his work. A great nose for news, Chip earned the respect of the entire staff.

Any editor with a half a brain knows a neighborhood murder sends chills through the reader's spine as he dashes for newsstands. Newspapers ride the drama. No matter what the polls report, good news will not sell newspapers. The *New York Times*, the *New York Post*, and the *Daily News* battled for the Westchester County circulation. The *Statesman* had to be better. The Vietnam War and the national news wore thin fast, so the hunt for local bad news was always in the forefront.

In 1967, Yonkers started to deteriorate. Neighborhoods changed overnight. Increased crime and drug traffic pushed the blue-collar homeowner to rural upstate. These were the children of immigrant parents who built the city and owned the homes. The hunt for good schools and safe neighborhoods kept residents moving. Those left behind would absorb declining conditions and wallow in despair.

The newspaper circulation fell off as city population decreased. For a short time we enjoyed plenty of readers, good stories, and a good news staff. Veteran reporters like Ellen Campion* always had good local stories.

Ellen, a native New Yorker and the paper's education writer, always plugged for front-page coverage and got it. Ellen's coverage of school news earned her high grades. A rail thin, sandy blonde with high cheekbones, Ellen, as a teen, had every boy in high school chasing her. This pretty blue-eyed Irish woman, now sixty, ran out of steady lovers later in life and never married.

A heavy drinker, Ellen had a polite charm about her—drunk or sober. The years of alcohol abuse took a toll on her once gorgeous skin. She still had enough appeal, however, in that graceful body to catch a glancing eye now and then. The rumor circulated that in her younger years, she dated the publisher, John Shields, which gave her a front-office connection.

The news meetings in the morning were torture. Martin listened and talked little. He favored a one-on-one talk more than group meetings. Twiddling thumbs and a blank stare often showed his displeasure with the meetings. After a short time we stopped them.

Martin began to show his true nature, being suspicious to the point of paranoia. A joke floated around that he read the newspaper and watched the newsroom staff at the same time. He had radar ears and it drove him almost insane to spot a group of reporters chatting. He never chewed anyone out, only walked by and stared to show his displeasure. He believed in a quick solution—firing.

At lunch one day he explained to Chip and me how to handle employees. "Fire one and the rest will straighten up." Martin strongly believed in the pink slip method of getting people's attention.

"Try it."

Martin did trust me. He didn't think I threatened his position and liked the idea of my staying away from the chat sessions. Martin disliked people in general. In private, he seldom had a kind word for anyone, and had few friends. He was a competent and talented editor, but he hated many ethnic groups.

Bigoted phrases were the norm. "That Jew and Spic have to go," and, "That Black is on his way out." He made these statements to me in the privacy of his office. I found it appalling to hear. A strange guy, I thought. I always wondered what he thought about Italians. However, he treated me with respect and kindness, at least to my face. His wife even brought a home-cooked dinner to our house after my wife gave birth to our second daughter, Carla.

We went to lunch in New York a few times and he gave me complete control over the newsroom. My reputation as a good, diligent worker paid off. I moved away from writing and more into directing news traffic. I enjoyed the status of a news manager. I buckled down and focused my all to put out a respectable *Yonkers Herald Statesman*.

There were plenty of newsworthy stories to choose from in Yonkers, more than in Florida. The reader's appetite for gory stories never changes. Geography has no impact on an appetite for revolting news. Regrettable it may be, but crime news is key to a newspaper's survival.

Chapter 16
Workplace Romances

Love can sometimes be magic, but magic can
sometimes ... just be an illusion.
—Javan

The workplace cultivates a fertile breeding ground for love affairs and rocky marriages. The *Yonkers Herald Statesman* had its share of both. Engaged Society Editor Florence Rizzo* and a married reporter, David Wallace*, had a love affair rivaling an awarding-winning soap opera.

The relationship started with small talk in the newsroom, a friendly Friday night drink at the Casa D'Roma, and ended up with secret night phone calls, morning motel lovemaking, and drugs. It brought one family to the brink of destruction. The two editors' fascinating love affair kept the newsroom gossip line humming. More juicy news floated around inside the newsroom than outside. Everyone wanted to know what went on. Few really cared about the people. The scandal, though, made delicious lunch chatter.

The late sixties began the Age of Aquarius and caution was thrown to the wind. Women burned their bras, walked topless on the beaches, and wanted the sexual freedom enjoyed by men. The activists opened the floodgates to emancipate uninhibited love.

The Graduate zoomed to number one at the movie box office. Vietnam War protesters pushed for peace and love. A majority of the youth enjoyed toying with drugs, resulting in a fatal attraction for many.

Pot smoking, acid dropping, cocaine snorting, and using other so-called recreational drugs made their way even into the newsrooms of America. The combination of drugs and extramarital love affairs muddied the waters of some of the nation's newsrooms. The *Herald Statesman* set its own stage for a steaming *affaire d'amour*. Florence Rizzo and David Wallace played the leading roles.

Florence and I hit it off immediately. Two New York Italians, we had much in common. The large, attractive, well–proportioned 25-year-old olive-skinned beauty with huge black eyes was a joy to look at. Florence and I enjoyed each other's company. We made it a must to stop for a glass of wine at the Casa D'Roma every Friday night. A generous and fun person, Florence had a wit I adored. We cared for each other, not as lovers, but as a close brother and sister relationship.

Never far from each other, we did so many things together that the staff got mixed signals. I made it clear we were never lovers, but warm, close friends. I found her vibrant and intelligent, not sexual. When she traveled to Manhattan on Saturday to shop, I went with her. When she wanted to go to lunch with a friend, I was ready to go. When she wanted to talk about something sensitive, she called me.

I frequently stopped at her mansion-like home in New Rochelle to have dinner and a few drinks. Her mother, a widow for ten years, always welcomed me like a son. The death of her father, a wealthy contractor, left Florence, like many fatherless children, empty, searching for a patriarchal figure. Maybe that is what she saw in me. She carried an unusual loneliness that never seemed to leave her. Living on the edge helped to suppress it.

Florence talked to me incessantly about her strange love affair with David. I listened but said little, and she liked it that way. It made little sense to get into the morality of it. She believed she was on the right path to happiness. As close as we were, Florence remained a puzzle.

Engaged to marry her college boyfriend, Mike James*, Florence suddenly turned her affection on Wallace. He was a happily married man, but David loved the attention and Florence's chemistry. They were both "free thinkers" and got a kick out of smoking pot together. The drugs calmed her, put her in a philosophical mood. Florence used me as an excuse to see him, which I didn't mind.

She invited her friends and I invited David to her house parties. She hoped the house filled with friends disguised the secret romance. The affair and a lifestyle change took its toll on me. I spent little time with my family and suddenly I went from a moderate drinker to a heavy hitter. I overflowed in the "good life."

Florence always bragged about her admiration for Timothy Leary, the college professor turned acidhead lecturer. Every time this crackpot came to New York, she begged me to go with her to hear him. I refused each time.

"You know I'd do anything for you, Florence, but don't ask me to sit a couple of hours and listen to that weirdo. I'm too square for that shit."

"He has so many philosophical things to say about the universe and our cosmos," she replied.

"Like drugs are okay."

She smiled, and went without me.

Florence's engagement to her college boyfriend confused even her closest friends. She planned a large wedding, picked out a beautiful white gown, the wedding party, and the date. And yet she relished her continuous love attachment with David. In the middle of the affair, she would remind me of the wedding.

"You're coming to my wedding, aren't you?" She repeated the question almost daily.

"Absolutely," I said for the twentieth time. "I'll be there and stand in line to dance with the bride."

Her black eyes lit up. "I can't wait, my Italian brother."

I thought about her dizzy affair with Wallace. Maybe she thought the fling would be short and disappear after a little fun—something to hold her lonely heart in place until marriage brought her that inner security. The affair, though, for her appeared to be more than a passing fancy. David wanted it short. He had a loyal wife, two adorable sons, and never planned leaving his family. He saw nothing long-term. Florence kept the love alive and put extra time into the romance.

A bright college student, Florence had graduated with honors from New York University. She did an admirable job as assistant society editor and wrote extremely well. She rated high on the promotions list at the paper, possibly in line for a newspaper executive job.

She had a passion for country music singers and idolized Johnny Cash. When Cash came to New York to shoot a CBS television special, Florence jumped on the chance to interview the budding star. Later she wanted to write a book about him. They became friends and she claimed to talk with Cash frequently on the phone. The Cash management loved the press connection to New York and the Gannett news chain. When Cash came in with the Statler Brothers, she went on the town with the brothers, only found them too friendly. One got extremely fresh with her.

I became acquainted with Mike, her future husband. Mike appeared to be unaware of Florence's liaison, and Florence seemed happy with this well-built, handsome, black haired, 26-year-old contractor. The three of us drank together at the Waterfront Café along the Hudson, listened to music, and talked about our dreams. Mike loved her very much and knew the guardian role I played with his future wife. I always made sure to let him know how happy I was for both of them.

"You're a lucky guy, Mike," I said. "You're getting a gorgeous and kind woman." I felt no qualms at saying such things to Mike because I believed that Florence would end the affair when the two of them were married.

He looked at me with a huge smile. "I know, and you better be there for the festivities,"

"Where else would I be that day?"

At the crowded wedding shower, Florence received an array of beautiful gifts, and then we toasted her for a healthy and long married life.

She thanked the guests and in turn lifted her gin and tonic above

her head. "If I had one wish, it would be eternal life for my friends."
She almost sobbed.

"Cheers," someone shouted.

"*Cent 'anni!*" another voice boomed. In Italian, *cent 'anni* means
a hundred years.

I walked over to Florence, hugged her, and kissed her on the
cheek. "What a beautiful night," I said.

"It's only the beginning," she responded.

"I know it is, sweetheart." I watched her and Mike head for the
door. I waved goodbye and walked over to the bar for a nightcap.

I sat alone and wondered why Florence meticulously put together
a fairy-tale wedding while on a collision course with disaster. An
ominous feeling came over me. I shivered. It was scary, like a fatal
sign. Bad vibes hovered nearby. I reached for the glass of white wine,
gulped it down, and walked out into the dark night.

Maybe I had too much to drink.

Chapter 17
A Passionate Bite out of Life

*Footfalls echo in the memory down the passage
which we did not take
Towards the door we never opened into the rose-
garden.*

—T.S. Eliot, "Four Quartets"

When I think about Florence Rizzo and others, with their office lovers, I think about Eliot's words. And there are times I take it a step further to a remark I once heard: "People take different roads seeking fulfillment and happiness. Just because they're not on your road doesn't mean they've gotten lost."

No matter what I thought, New Rochelle's Florence, exuding restless beauty, was hell bent on balancing her unique love life.

She knew the high wire act carried danger. Driven by her insatiable passion, Florence accepted her fate knowing she couldn't play her love game for long and certainly not alone. She needed help and found it by playing Cupid.

Her closest friend was petite, forty-year-old Jill Levine*, a part-time copy editor, who longed for a tender romance, too. Jill and Florence loved to double date, hoping it would throw off nosy staff members. *Friends getting together*, Florence called it. The cover-up never fooled anyone. I'm sure managing editor, Bob Martin, became suspicious of the groups, but the unwritten policy that banned office romances went unchallenged.

Jill towered four feet high in her unbalanced frame. Born with a spinal defect, she walked with a slight limp, and had a noticeable hunched back. Despite an awkward build, her jet-black hair, deep-set black eyes, and baby doll stature gave her an incredibly attractive appearance. With a small round face, this Jewish beauty resembled a young Elizabeth Taylor. Clever and quick on her feet, Jill had a wit and a carefree sense of humor that made her extremely popular.

She had a long connection with newspapers. As a teen, she worked at the defunct *New York Mirror* where she met her husband, Steve, who at that time, worked for *Star Magazine*. Her well-attended Jewish wedding drew raves from her friends. Her children attended Westchester County's finest Jewish schools. After the two sons' Bar Mitzvahs, Jill decided to work part time at the *Herald Statesman* and enjoy the freshness of an outside job.

A Hunter College graduate with a major in economics, Jill wrote an excellent business column that drew a large readership. She had only one heartthrob in her life, Steve, a devoted husband, who gave her love, security, and stability. *What wife could ask for more?* Her marriage appeared destined to last a lifetime.

Like a spoiled, uncontrollable teenager with wanderlust, she wanted more. Jill started to look when her one love wore thin and monotonous. Obsessed by curiosity and sensual drive, Jill searched for another fulfilling bite out of life.

"I don't want to let the rest of my life slip by without an exhilarating love affair," she told a close friend. "I want a love that is not complicated or a threat to my marriage. I want a brief, deep love affair on my own terms," she said. Excited and intrigued by what she saw in other newsroom encounters, she plunged ahead.

"Time for my dessert," she giggled.

Jill found what she searched for in handsome, slender, and smart Bill Blair*, another married copy editor. He was a heavy drinker, a womanizer, and a regular at Florence's house parties. Blair, an Irish guy with sleepy blue eyes, played the field and expected little in return.

The childless couple lived in White Plains, about 20 miles north of Yonkers. Bill's wife, Sharon*, a closet drinker and a loner, rarely attended any social functions. Introduced to her at the company's Christmas party, I found her attractive, but somber and withdrawn.

"You're Bill's drinking buddy, aren't you?" She held out her hand.

I smiled and shook her soft hand. "We have a few once in a while after work."

"What does he do with the rest of his time?"

"You'll have to ask him," I replied, still smiling.

"I have and I can't get a straight answer," she said.

I began to squirm and quickly changed the subject.

"How do you like White Plains?"

"I hate it," she said, staring away in the direction of her husband. "Nice meeting you, Carl." She turned her back on me and slowly walked, with a drink in hand, over to the far corner of the hall to sit at an empty table.

A sadness came over me as I watched her fidget in her chair. Uncomfortable with the noisy crowd, she wanted to be alone.

Bill was an experienced forty-two-year-old news editor and former crime reporter. At the end of the workday, he made the "Irish Shanty Bar and Grill," two blocks from the newspaper, his watering hole. You could find him there every night. At times he stayed overnight in a motel. Bill looked amazingly well, considering his heavy, daily drinking.

I spent my share of happy hours with Bill and listened to him lament his unhappy married life and his fresh affair with Jill. Bill, a person who couldn't keep a secret, detailed his first lovemaking session with Jill.

"It started with a few drinks with her and Florence one night, and before you know it, Jill and I were making love in her car." Bill looked down and twirled the straw in his large, frosted Martini glass.

"I was surprised that such a short relationship produced quick results," he said.

"Just like that?" I said.

"Yeah, just like that," he answered.

"You gotta be kidding me. Wouldn't it make sense to go to a

motel? Making love in a car is gross. You're not a high school kid," I said. "How could you even enjoy such lovemaking?"

He shrugged his shoulders, finished the drink in front of him and tapped the empty glass on the bar, signaling the bartender for another drink.

"I've been around a lot of women," he said. "When they are ready to go, they are ready to go. Whether it's in a car, at the movies, or in the office, when they are ready, you move in." He smiled, a hint of lurking satisfaction in his eyes. "Did you know there is more screwing in company offices than whorehouses?"

"Are those official statistics or Bill's bullshit?" I joked.

"We're getting off course here," he said as a smile spread over his face.

"Let me tell you the whole story." He frowned at his near-empty glass "I left my car at home Friday, and Jill volunteered to drive me home. My wife didn't think it was wrong and neither did Jill's husband. Giving a fellow worker a ride home is purely acceptable."

"Perfectly acceptable," I echoed.

"She pulled up under a tree on a dark road about two blocks from my house. Thanks. I reached over and gave her a thank you kiss on the cheek and in a flash, she moved her lips against mine and grabbed ..."

"You don't have to get into the nitty-gritty," I said. "I'm convinced."

"Do me a favor and keep this conversation to yourself," he said.

"Who am I going to tell, your wife?" I joked.

"Not funny," he said.

"Florence and David know that we are caught up in dizzy screwed-up love affairs," he said. I was surprised how quickly he downed his drink.

"Slow down on the sauce, or you won't have a love life to screw up," I said.

He put his lower lip on his front teeth, wiped his mouth with his thumb and finger. "Does it matter?"

He was getting drunk and confused. *It's time to go,* I thought. I sat close enough to him to get a good look at his weary blue eyes.

"If you want to kill yourself, trade that glass in for a gun. It's faster," I said.

He nodded his head and closed his eyes while remaining silent. Then, he changed the subject. "Florence is having a party Friday night. Are you planning on going?"

"Of course, I never miss them."

"It's the last one before her wedding," he said "Everyone is going to be there."

"Should be interesting," I said as we departed toward home for the night.

Chapter 18
Firing the Sports Editor

He who joyfully marches in rank and file has already earned my contempt. He has been given a large brain by mistake, since for him the spinal cord would suffice.
—Albert Einstein

I walked into the office Saturday morning in no mood for a talk with Bob Martin about our Sports Editor. With a giant hangover after a wild Friday night, I had no yearning to talk about Dave Kaminer or anyone else. Peace and quiet, survive through the day, and trek homeward—those were my goals, pure and simple. *Forget it.* My chances of working serenely at my desk were about equal to hitting an inside straight.

Martin grabbed me the minute I walked into the office. "I fired Dave Kaminer." His voice bounced off my aching head, but I got the message. Martin didn't go into details. He didn't have to. The fact that he disliked Dave with a passion was obvious. Dave was Jewish and Bob constantly hurled ethnic slurs about him around the office. A week later David's assistant and Jewish friend, David Bicofsky, left before he had a chance to get fired.

After Martin fired Kaminer, an empty sports department stared me in the face. Martin called me in his office. "I need your help to put out the sport pages," he said. I could tell he was still fuming, "I know you worked in sports in Florida and the two of us can get this thing out."

We finally put the sports section to bed. "You did me a great favor and I won't forget it," Bob said.

I nodded my head and headed at a snail's pace back to my desk.

Martin had been in a firing mood lately. The Saturday before, he fired police reporter Archie O'Neill*. Martin found Archie sleeping on his desk, loaded with alcohol and drugs.

Bob wanted to throw him out physically, but Archie left on his own. He tumbled out the door and into the street. Archie, a bright police reporter, went to work for a travel magazine. After I left the newspaper, Martin hired him back.

I never heard from Dave Kaminer again, but I did hear David Bicofsky got a copy editor's niche at the *Record* in Hackensack, New Jersey.

Editor Barney Waters did not interfere with Martin's wild decision to fire the sports editor. Waters, who headed the news department, wrote bland editorials and stayed out of newsroom operations and out of trouble. He wanted me to write a feature story on my lung operation. I refused and told him it was too private. Add that to mistakes I have made. I decided later to write the story, but I left the newspaper before I had a chance to complete it.

Waters did what I thought was an admirable piece of journalism, an idea he adapted from the *Miami Herald*, titled "Know Your Neighbor." The series shot up the readership numbers for the *Herald*.

Barney titled our string of tales, "They Live Among Us." The stories told about the Mafia families living in Westchester County and the mob ties to New York City. The newspaper had front-page photos of the Mafia homes and even named family members including wives, daughters, and sons. The series even named schools the children attended.

The newspaper phones rang off the hook. Waters thought he did a great job. The threats got so bad that a county judge issued Waters a special gun permit.

Waters never got specific about the calls, but it was clear that the small fish in the Mafia tried, to little avail, to rough him. After a few months, the ordeal died down.

The *Statesman* also ran a Christmas story on how charitable people are during the Yule season. One of our reporters dressed as a beggar and stood on the corner asking for money. I heard Waters' wife approached one of the disguised reporters and scolded him for begging.

"Get a job" she cried. The story, repeated by several other newspapers, drew good readership and laughter from the newsroom.

The newspaper did few investigative stories, satisfied to stay on course reporting the local news. Like all the Gannett newspapers in Westchester County, the emphasis on soft local news took precedent. It worked until the neighborhoods changed in Yonkers and Mount Vernon. Circulation dropped dramatically, forecasting the beginning of the end.

Chapter 19
A Chest X-Ray Reveals
Shocking Results

There are moments when everything goes well; don't
be frightened, it won't last.
　　　　　—Jules Renard

Life for me had become moments of joy. My career reached a new peak, my family lived in an ideal community, I loved the New York City area, and adored new friends. It was a time like no other I had ever experienced, and trouble was the last thing I expected.

On a gorgeous October day in 1968, Terry Moore, a reporter, and I went to lunch at the North Broadway deli and enjoyed delicious roast beef on a bun and a soda. Returning along Wilder Street, I saw a Westchester County mobile X-ray unit parked nearby. A short line of people waited to get a free X-ray. I hadn't had a chest X-ray since I left Florida. Why not now? "Let's get a free X-ray," I said.

Terry gazed at the large white van, which reflected a noticeable glare from the autumn sun. He hesitated. "I don't know." His voice was a bit on the weak side. "I'm always frightened of X-rays. I rarely go to a doctor. If something is wrong with me, I don't want to know. I found out, too, that even if there's nothing wrong with you, the doctors will find something."

I laughed. "Haven't you heard of preventative medicine?" I asked. "I'm sure you know that early detection could save your life."

"Of course." He appeared to be most uncomfortable as we drew close to the mobile unit. He stopped for a few seconds and rubbed his chin. "Okay, okay, you sold me. Let's get an X-ray."

We both climbed into the little unit, took our X-rays and forgot about them.

Three days later and two weeks before the big party at Florence's house, I received a phone call from my family physician, Dr. Robert Bentley. At eight o'clock at night, I was surprised to hear the doctor's voice.

"Westchester County X-ray Unit Medical Group called me and said a dark shadow appeared on your right lung. They would like you to have a retake."

My heart began to race like crazy. I thought I was having a heart attack. Before I could say a word, he went on.

"Probably nothing," he said, trying to set me at ease.

"Sure, doctor, I'll do it as soon as possible."

When I hung up, numbness took over my body. *What the hell is going on?* Then, I tried to dismiss it. *He's right, probably nothing.*

We were wrong. The second X-ray showed the same shadow. Dr. Bentley scheduled an appointment for me with a pulmonary surgeon, Dr. Anthony Scholer.

"You have a grapefruit size bleb on your right lung," Dr. Scholer

"I don't know if it's malignant or not, but if we don't get it out, that lung could collapse and cause all sorts of problems."

I cleared my dry throat and thought this must a bad dream. I remained silent for a few seconds staring at the large X-ray of my lungs in front of me. The dark images made little sense to me. I would have to trust the doctor. "When do you want to do the operation?" The low, faint voice didn't even sound like me.

"The sooner, the better." The grim face looking at me was scary. "It's Friday night and I can schedule the surgery for Monday morning."

I wiped my sweaty forehead with my handkerchief, and fixed my eyes on the X-ray. "Okay. Monday will be fine." *Monday or any day wouldn't be fine to cut me open.*

"I'm going to admit you Sunday for some prep work."

Still in a fog, I nodded my head. The operation would take place in the North Tarrytown Hospital, the same hospital in which my daughter, Carla, was born a year earlier.

My wife, stunned and a nervous wreck, called my father, my sisters, and brother to explain about the surgery. They all wanted to be there.

In a robot's voice that matched my feelings, I called Managing Editor Bob Martin.

"I hope everything goes well and don't worry. We'll hold the fort down until you get back." He said my job was secure.

When you're told you have a life-threatening condition and must face major surgery, your mind spins in every direction. Bewilderment, anger, and fear bombard and fight for first place in your brain. You struggle to remain composed. What is taken for granted now becomes so precious. You think of your family, you pray for help, you try rationalize it, and then you confront it.

Lying on my back on the operating table, half in a daze, I waited for the anesthesia to take hold. A few days earlier I felt in the best of health, walking around, planning to spend a quiet weekend with my family. Now, I thought, here I am gazing at the bright lights above me as I wait for this major lung operation. *You never know, you never know,* I thought as my thinking process slowed down.

Well, let's get it over with. That's the last I remember as I drifted into a deep, peaceful sleep.

Waking up in the recovery room, I felt pain like I'd never encountered. The painkillers weren't strong enough. I forgot where I was until I looked up and saw a nurse patting my arm.

"It's all over," she said. "Everything went fine. The doctor will be in to talk to you in a minute, and then we will let you see your family."

I had so much pain running through my body, I had trouble understanding her.

Still in a fog, I vaguely saw the doctor walk in.

"Everything went extremely well." He looked under my white sheet to check the blood-soaked stitching that circled under my arm.

"No cancer," he said with a smile. "And I am going to increase the painkiller."

I took a long sigh of relief and waited for the rest. Doctors always follow good news with bad news.

"You're going to be a pretty sore for a long time, and we have to watch that lung for a couple of years to see if the bubbles we took off don't return and collapse the lung. Other than that, you should be out of the hospital in a couple of days and back to work in a few weeks." He looked at me as if to be sure I understood. "I'll let you see your family now," he said.

When you're sick, there is no better medicine than family. Seeing the entire family together gave me a bolt of energy.

We hugged and kissed each other for five minutes, and my wife had tears in her eyes. "I knew you'd make it. You're a tough guy, and we were all praying for you."

The next night, six members of the news staff somehow got by the nurse's desk with a bottle of gin and a six-pack of beer. Delighted as I was to see the staff, I was flabbergasted at the amount of booze they smuggled in. I did join in to have one drink and then two more. Risky, but fun, since I had a large amount of painkillers in my body.

Then the conversation turned somber. "We were worried sick about you," Florence said. "One minute you're talking about my party and the next minute, I get the terrible news that you're in the hospital. You scared the crap of us." She stopped talking long enough to take a breath. "Are you going to be okay?"

Everyone in the room remained silent waiting for me to answer.

Jill and Bill, holding hands, came closer to my bed.

"I can answer that question in one word—yes."

Yes said it all, so we chatted about other things. The drinks just about flattened me. "Enough," I said. "Any more booze and they'll take me back to the operating room."

I was too sick and tired to talk anymore. It was time for the company to leave. Florence, trailing the rest of the staff, reached over to kiss me on the check. "Get healthy."

She spoke over her shoulder and winked.

"You're still coming to my wedding aren't you?"

Half asleep, I nodded my head.

I smiled and she disappeared down the hospital hallway.

Chapter 20
Going South

After two weeks of physical therapy, playing with a beach ball, and eventually walking two miles a day, I was eager and physically ready to go back to work.

"You're a good patient, and you heal fast," Doctor Jacobsen said as he examined the thirty-stitch incision that circled under my right arm.

"I'm going to ease up on the painkillers before you get to like them too much." The corners of his mouth turned up in a half-smile.

"You're going to be sore for a while, but you're like a horse ready to break out of the starting gate," he said. "I don't think I could hold you out of work much longer.

"We'll take another X-ray to make sure. Then I'll release you to go back to work. Don't forget, though. Get an X-ray once a year."

Pale and still haggard, I started back on the copy desk with a welcome-back group around me. Not much had changed. Bob Martin acted as paranoid as ever, and the office love affairs soared at their usual torrid pace.

Chip Miller finally got my attention with hand gestures. "Let's have lunch today. I have something confidential to tell you."

"Love to. Let's go next door to Casa D'Roma, I want to say hello to my friend, Phil Gato. I haven't seen him since my operation."

"He's a super bartender. He asks about you whenever I'm in the place."

I noticed Bob Martin watching us from his office. He stared, biting on his cigar.

After Chip left, Martin came over to my desk. "It's great to have you back. I finally got someone in the newsroom I can trust. Keep Friday open and we'll go down to the city and eat some Spanish food."

"A bunch of free lunches are coming my way," I said.

"What you've gone through, you deserve them." He returned to his office with a quick glance back at the working staff.

Florence came over and whispered, "Are you well enough to come over tonight?"

"Are you kidding me? I can barely work. I'll take a rain check," I said.

"I don't give rain checks," she snapped, probably upset at the tone of my voice.

I didn't want to make a scene in the middle of the newsroom. "Don't get crazy on me," I said. "I need a few days rest."

She wanted to hold a party and invite David, Bill, and Jill.

"I'd love to, but give me a chance to mend a little."

Impatient Florence wanted things to happen right away. She finally composed herself and said. "Okay, how's Friday?"

"Friday's out. I'm having dinner with Bob Martin."

"Saturday night at 8 o'clock, and don't be late."

I grinned, ignoring her snide remark. "Unless I wind up back in the hospital, I'll be there," I said.

She smiled after getting her own way and walked away.

Chip showed up next. "Let's get going, it's lunch time,"

Ever so slowly, I pulled myself out of the desk chair, put on my suit jacket, and walked out with Chip. All eyes in the newsroom were fixed on us.

Walking toward the restaurant, I asked Chip about his confidential story.

"Wait until we find a table." Chip headed for a table in a far corner.

Once seated, I leaned toward him. "Come on, Chip, I'm dying of curiosity, what the hell is going on?"

"You need to be sitting down for the news.

"I'm resigning this afternoon," he said.

"You're what?" I said as though I hadn't heard him.

"You heard me. I'm quitting and going back to Orlando. Kathy hates it here. If I stay another month, I won't have a wife. The *Orlando Sentinel* offered me a political writer's job and I accepted."

I told him how disappointed I was to see him leave, but his family comes first.

"I'm sure you made the right decision," I said, "I'll miss you, to put it mildly."

I knew there was more to Chip's resignation than he wanted to admit. One of the reporters had a crush on him and he was afraid that temptation might overcome him. Chip, an extremely religious guy, thought it would better to leave than get involved with Carol Martino*, a beautiful, black-haired, brown-eyed general assignment reporter from Rome, New York. Heads always turned when she walked though the newsroom. A college-age beauty, she loved Chip's Southern politeness and mannerisms. Chip ran and Carol chased. He knew it would be only a matter of time before he crumbled and they headed for bed. I had a feeling Kathy knew and pushed Chip harder to leave Yonkers.

"The hardest part is telling Bob Martin," he said. "He makes me a little uncomfortable."

"The worst he can do is fire you." I laughed at my own joke. "Don't worry about him." I said. "I know he respects you, but he doesn't care who leaves."

He looked a little relieved. After all, he was the one who called me to Yonkers. Ironic that he should be going back to Orlando. I imagine he felt a sense of guilt.

"Are you happy here?" he asked.

"I love it. This is where I want to be, for a long time."

I have learned, though, that nothing, and I mean nothing goes as we plan. As soon as you get comfortable, something goes haywire. "Life has so many quick, sharp turns, it's impossible to know where you'll be tomorrow, much less next week."

"How right you are," he said. His face took on a pensive look.

"I hate to see you go. I'm not upset, however, that you called me here and now you're leaving." I didn't tell him how much I really would miss him. "I want to thank you. It's what the family and I wanted."

After lunch, I watched Chip go to Bob Martin's office to hand in his resignation.

Newspapers treat resignations with little concern. Hundreds of candidates wait to take your place, and some work for almost nothing. Management knows there is no shortage of help. Journalism schools unwisely pump out thousands of applicants every year for a handful of jobs.

The news about Chip's leaving spread fast. Barney Waters, the editor who rarely visited the newsroom, came in to talk to Chip. No amount of persuasion could change his mind.

The buzz now would be about a going away party for Chip. The domino effect appeared to be taking place as two reporters resigned right after Chip.

Theasa Toohey, a brilliant reporter and an average wire editor, headed for the Detroit Free Press. She worked next to me on the copy desk and we became friends. I remember her claiming she had the "best set of legs in the newsroom." I never argued with her about that. Theasa never came to any of parties, and I had little contact with her outside the newspaper. With her talent, I knew she would find a great job.

The other reporter, Mary Stevens*, an average reporter who covered Yonkers City Hall, found a new home at Associated Press. When Mary told me her she was assigned to the Fargo, North Dakota, bureau, I almost fainted.

"New York for North Dakota is not what I would call a favorable trade," I said with a smile.

She had a confusing love life. Mary fell in love with a married Yonkers policeman, an unwise emotional move. Pat Patrick*, a Yonkers native, was a six-foot, four- inch, good-looking Irishman. A staunch Catholic, he had no intentions of leaving his wife. Pat wanted Mary but not long-term. She told me that he slept in the back seat of her car as she drove to Fargo. He spent a lot of time with her but the affair headed nowhere. She eventually went to the AP Tampa bureau and married.

With the changes taking place in the newsroom, strong vibrations sent signals of transformation.

I don't know, maybe things were going too well.

Chapter 21
A Parting of Friends

A few selected news staff workers received an invitation to Chip Miller's going away party. The gathering possibly set a record for the shortest sendoff ever. Every two minutes or so, Chip glanced at his wristwatch with a nervous eye. He never stayed long at any social event. Mingling socially appeared to give him a weird sense of guilt.

Carol Martino sat close to Chip and gazed at him with misty eyes, apparently mesmerized by his blond, boyish looks. She sipped on an iced gin and tonic, looking as if she could easily cry. She knew this would be the last night they would see each other. The two agreed no more communications after tonight. Time to break it off.

"I can't stay long," Chip said, "I have to finish packing. We leave at six o'clock in the morning."

Too shy to sit close to Carol, Chip inched away. Carol moved closer and whispered in his ear. He cracked his stern appearance and smiled.

"Would you excuse us for a few minutes?" Carol said as she grabbed her jacket as Chip stood up.

"Fine party this is," Florence said. "The honored guest has a half of glass of beer and decides to leave."

"Let them go," I said, "There's just more for us to drink."

Without saying a word, Carol and Chip hurried out the door.

"Where are they off to?" Florence's assumed innocence didn't quite make it with me. Her eyes sparkled with amusement and approval.

"My bet is Carol's apartment," Jill said.

"Who cares?" I said.

"He better come back. I didn't get a chance say goodbye," David said.

With the music playing, Jill and Bill decided to dance, and Florence and David followed.

I sat alone, staring into the amber liquid inside my glass, a little depressed about Chip's leaving. He had been such a good friend, but I knew he had to go. His guilt about Carol gave him little rest, and left him feeling out of control. He wanted to make amends to his wife.

Three hours later, the restaurant door opened and there stood Carol and Chip. Everyone remained silent. Carol, her long black hair hiding part of her face, came and sat at our table. Chip remained standing.

"Time to go," he said. "Thanks to all of you for the party."

He shook hands, hugged some of the staff, and looked over at me with a signal to meet him outside.

I nodded my head and walked out the door with Chip right behind me.

Near his car, he held out his hand. I shook it and hugged him. It was a heartfelt time for both of us.

Chip had trouble getting out words. "It's been a pleasure, and I hope we see each other again."

"I'm going to miss you." I looked at him and got sort of a lump in my throat. "If I get to Florida, I'll give you call."

"You do that," he said as he climbed into his car.

"Keep in touch," I yelled as his car slowly moved away. I knew he wouldn't.

Chip's car backed up. He rolled the window down and spoke with a big smile spread across his face. "Nothing happened, believe me."

"I believe you." I watched as he slowly drove away.

Once again inside the restaurant, I spotted Carol at one of the empty tables. She wore dark glasses to hide her tears. When I reached her, she took off her glasses and looked up with a tearful smile. "It was a lot fun."

"Chip's a pretty straight guy," I said. "He would never leave his wife."

Carol nodded her head in agreement. "Chip thinks if he cheats on her he would burn in hell."

"It's more than that," I said. "His love and respect for her is deeply rooted inside him.

She made no reply.

"The temptation bothers him. Chip wants to be the perfect husband." I softened my voice. "Humans make plenty of mistakes."

"Was his love for me a mistake?" Carol asked.

"How could it be?" I said, leaving her question hanging. "I'm convinced he will never leave her side again." I paused to carefully choose my words. "Yeah, he is a religious guy, and I am sure he felt guilty being with you. Now he'll do his penance." I grabbed my jacket and fumbled in my pocket, looking for my car keys.

After saying farewell to the staff, Carol walked over and kissed me on the cheek. "You're right; he's never going to leave home again." Tossing her long hair back and putting her hands in her leather jacket, she walked out the door and disappeared into the summer night.

There would be no consoling her. Carol would live through her obsession with Chip. Such a beautiful woman, her important years were ahead her. This charming twenty-year-old would meet other Chips and her prince charming one day. Chip belonged to Carol's yesterdays and not her tomorrows.

Carol did not stay much longer in Yonkers. She quit and went back to Rome, New York. I never heard from her again.

Chapter 22
The Road to Hackensack

*He that leaves nothing to chance will do a few things
wrong, but he will do very few things.*
—George Savile, Marquess de Halifax

That Tuesday started out like any other working day until Bob
Martin stopped by my desk. "I'd like you to work on the *Mount
Vernon Argus* copy desk a couple days a week." It wasn't a request.
It was an order.

The Mount Vernon newspaper was part of the Westchester chain
printed in Yonkers. I helped put it together almost every day. Since
I was changing headlines and cutting stories in the production
department, it did make sense to have me work in the main office a
few days a week.

The editor, about to retire, would leave a top job opening, and I
could campaign for it. The newspaper, smaller than the *Statesman,*
had lost circulation in the past year and appeared to be sliding into
oblivion. Although caught in a population shift, it did provide an
excellent challenge for a young editor.

Even though I really didn't have a choice, I agreed to work in
Mount Vernon in the hope it would lead to better things. It didn't.
The editor retired and the assistant editor got the promotion. My job
would remain the same, working on two newspapers.

I decided as long as I was working hard, I should get more money.
I asked for a raise.

"I know you deserve it." Martin leaned back in his office chair, biting on his cigar. "I'll get back to you in a week with an answer."

The week went by with no word from Martin; I walked in his office. "Did you hear anything on my raise yet?"

"Yeah, ten dollars," he said. "Not much, but something."

I didn't say a word. He knew I was disappointed.

"Don't worry. There will be more," he said. "If it were up to me, I'd give you one hundred dollars more a week, but I do what they tell me." I knew Bob would not go to bat for me. His only loyalty was to himself.

"Thanks." I walked out of the office hot under the collar. After work, I headed for the Casa D'Roma next door, intending to drink my anger away.

Drinking at the bar alone, I talked to myself. *I work my tail off for the newspaper and get shit for it.* I jumped when I felt a hand on my shoulder. "You look like you lost your best friend." I was startled, wrapped up in my own world. It was Jill.

"Bad day. Where's Bill?"

"He'll be here. A little more work left."

Then, "Come join us." I could tell by the lilt in her voice and light in her eyes that Bill had walked in.

Breaching one of my staunchest codes, *don't drink and talk about personal affairs,* I told the two about my meeting with Bob Martin.

"Those ungrateful sons of bitches," she said.

Bill shook his head, a look of disgust on his face. "You are one of the best workers around here. Tell them to shove the job up their ass."

"Only one problem with that." I let out a big sigh. "I know this sounds weird, but I like it here. And I would never quit a job without having another. Don't forget I have a family that depends on me."

"You know they're hiring at the *Bergen Record* in Hackensack, New Jersey," Bill said. "Carl Jellenhouse is one of the editors there. Give him a call and find out what they have to offer."

I ordered another drink. "No, it's a little too far to travel. I live in Dobbs Ferry and Hackensack is thirty miles away."

"Just a thought." Bill shrugged his shoulders.

The next day, Martin called me in his office. I thought he had a change of heart.

Wrong! "I wanted you to know we hired a City Editor—Dick Harrison."

"Great," I said. "Is that all?"

"Dick will be working with you." Bob chomped on his cigar.

"Now I know," I said in a curt tone and walked out. *They have money to hire another editor, but not enough to give me a decent raise. Screw 'em.* Fuming, I walked down the stairs to the lobby telephone booth and called the *Record* in Hackensack. I asked for Carl Jellenhouse. I hoped my voice didn't reflect my inner turmoil.

Surprise! He came on the line immediately. "Send me your resume. I'll get back to you," he said in a joyful tone.

And to be sure, that's exactly what I did. A few days later, I got a call at my house from Jellenhouse. "I took a good look at your resume, and I like what I see. Are you still interested in working for the *Record*?"

"Yes, I am," I said.

I wanted to know more about what I was getting into.

"Why don't you come over, and we can discuss it," he said. "I'll transfer you to my secretary, and she'll set up an appointment that suits both of us. Okay?"

I thanked him and could hardly wait to meet him face to face.

"I'm sure we can work something out."

The same feeling surged through me that I felt when I was leaving Florida. Something was about to happen.

The appointment was for Friday afternoon and I had to give the newspaper an excuse. I made up a doctor's appointment. I told my family about my plans and everyone looked worried. *Am I making the right move? Are we going to move to Jersey? What about school?*

The decision to stay in Dobbs Ferry answered the family's question. It would mean two-hour's traveling time, tolls, gas, plus wear-and-tear on the car—driving down the Saw Mill River Parkway, Henry Hudson Parkway, over the George Washington Bridge to Hackensack. I had to figure all that into my salary request. After our interview, Jellonhouse made a generous offer.

"I think this place is for you. Plenty of chances for advancement. The benefits are out of this world. We are a family-owned newspaper and able to offer more." The sales pitch was hitting home.

"Let me think about it for about a week."

"I'll look forward to hearing from you." I liked his smile.

A couple of the newspapers tucked under my arm, I headed for home. The paper appeared to be nothing but another bedroom community newspaper, no fancy frills, and plenty of ads.

Chip had told me his friend from North Carolina, Jerry Bellune, worked at the *Record,* and loved it there. Bellune had worked at Yonkers and left because he missed too many deadlines. *He's too good for this place,* I thought. I talked with Jerry and he did give the *Record* high grades.

To me, everything appeared in place. I thought about it and talked to Jill and Bill. I didn't talk to Florence or any other staff members.

"Take it," Jill seemed to be enthusiastic.

"Think it over carefully," countered Bill. "It's a big move."

It's the first time they disagreed on anything to my knowledge. I couldn't understand why Jill pushed for me to go. Maybe she really cared, but I found out differently later.

After a week of agonizing, I resigned from the *Statesman* and severed my ties to the Gannett newspaper chain. I had reservations, but I decided to chance it, like the chances I'd taken all my life. I didn't feel comfortable, but I knew I had to go. I hadn't reached my journey's end yet.

And I reassured myself with Savile's quote: *He that leaves nothing to chance will do few things wrong, but he will do very few things.*

Chapter 23
Last Days at the
Herald Statesman

The best of us are molded out of our faults.
—Shakespeare

"You're resigning." The words were correct, but his tone of voice denied it. "Why?"

I had shocked Bob Martin. *Great!* Moments before, I handed him a one sentence resignation effective in two weeks.

"I'm leaving the *Statesman* headed toward a much better paying job and a chance for advancement."

Bob's curiosity got the best of him. "You're going where?"

"The *Bergen Record* in Hackensack."

"Hackensack?" I didn't miss the sound of scorn.

"Yeah, Hackensack, New Jersey."

"A big mistake," he said. "A mistake you'll regret for a long time. You're going to be driving sixty miles a day and pay tolls, not to mention the rest of the traffic headaches."

"I'll be compensated for that," I said, noting his concern. For the first time since I met Martin, I detected honesty in his voice. He reached over and waved the resignation in front of my face. "I'll tear it up if you want me to."

"No, Bob. I appreciate your concern, but I think it's going to be great for me." I emphasized my words without raising my voice. "Shit—you guys won't give me a suitable raise, and now you're worried about my welfare? I'm ready to go."

"Okay," he said. "I'll start processing your resignation."

"Thanks for everything, Bob. I loved working here."

I walked out in the newsroom, a little numb, but relieved, like someone had lifted a heavy load from my shoulder. The word spread so fast that I hardly had a chance to sit down when Editor Barney Waters came out. "Are you sure you want to go?" I knew he wanted me to stay, but it was too late.

"I'm sure."

"Okay. Good luck to you." He made a swift exit from my desk and into his office.

With a gloomy look, Florence moved closer to me. "We'll still see you, won't we?"

"I'm not leaving the area, simply changing jobs." I knew what she was going to say next. "Yes, I'm coming to your wedding."

Her black eyes brightened and she smiled. "You always know what's on my mind." She moved toward her desk.

Jill and Bill came over. "Good for you. That's what they deserve."

"See you guys after work for a quick one,"

"A quick what?" Jill quipped.

By the end of the day everyone got the word and my last days at the Yonkers ticked away.

My going-away party was attended by no more than five staff members. I would keep in touch with them.

The last day I worked for the *Statesman*, Martin called me. Down to the final minute, he believed I'd change my mind. "I can still tear up your resignation."

I smiled. "Thanks for your confidence in me, but it's a little late."

"It's never too late."

"For me it is. I'm resolved and believe I'm making the right move."

"Enough said. Good luck."

I shook his hand and he looked at me with sadness in his eyes. He knew we would never work together again. I think he was hurt because he had lost someone he could trust. With Chip gone and now me, he'd likely not find a friendly face in the newsroom.

There was nothing more to say, or do.

It was time to go. Folding my jacket over my arm, I pulled my umbrella from under my desk where it must have been for a year or so. I walked down the stairs and past the guard, opening the huge steel door. As I stepped into the open air, I heard a resounding thud. The metal doors closed, never to open for me again.

As I moved toward my car in the parking lot, I walked in front of a couple of factory workers and overhead them chatting. "I understand Otis Elevator is going to close its doors here."

"Where the hell are they going to go, China?"

"Yeah, like everything else."

"Leave it up to the greedy corporate assholes to save a buck. They can always find somebody to do the job cheaper."

I watched the pair disappear up the street. As I drove out of parking lot, my eyes were fixed on the *Yonkers Herald Statesman*. Otis Elevator stood tall behind the newspaper. Like a mighty icon looking down from its tower, its final chapter would soon be written into Yonkers archives.

I always perceived Otis as unmovable, the same way I thought of my stay in Yonkers.

Chapter 24
A Short Stay that
Lasted Too Long

The only real mistake is the one from which we learn nothing.
—John Powell

My initial impression of the *Bergen Record* faded quickly. After a few months, I soured on the average bedroom community newspaper that covered Bergen County and a few other outlying New Jersey counties.

The newspaper turned out to be the biggest disappointment of my newspaper career. It reeked with management paranoia combined with ass kissing. Assistant editors were trampling over each other to reach the top. It was a living nightmare.

"Sad," a fellow copy editor remarked. "Every day, assistant editors can't wait to talk about the faults of other editors to the Executive Editor Carl Jellenhouse." I never understood why Jellenhouse tolerated the backbiting, and then later I thought that maybe he encouraged it.

The newspaper, a 20-minute ride from the George Washington Bridge, proved to be my biggest mistake. For me, it was the bottom of the well.

The chemistry wasn't there between my boss, Chief Copy Editor Bob Cummings, and me. We almost came to blows.

At first he was extremely friendly. "I am delighted to get an experienced copy editor. We have a lot of shit working here."

After that kind remark, our relationship plunged. He continued to find things wrong with headlines and copy. Cummings, a *Cincinnati Enquirer* transplant, was a big man with silver hair who was a bundle of nerves. Twitching, he never stood still and always found time to criticize any member of the copy desk.

I knew few people there. I worked midnight to seven in the morning and it was pure torture. After the first month, I was ready to quit, but I had nowhere to go. I even called Bob Martin for my old job back at the *Statesman.*

"I can't do it," he said. "Barely hanging on myself." It would be the last time I would speak to him. Martin did get fired and headed back to the Midwest where he came from, I heard. I think he became a public relation spokesperson for a politician.

After a few more months, I talked to Jellenhouse and he said that Cummings had complaints about me.

"We'll never get along," I said. Jellenhouse sided with Cummings.

It didn't matter. I was smothering and I had decided to quit, whatever happened. Walking out the door of the *Bergen Record* after resigning, I took a deep breath, one of the most refreshing of my life.

My short stay at the *Record* lasted too long.

Walking to my car in the parking lot, a fellow copy editor caught up with me. "Try the *Hudson Dispatch* in Union City [New Jersey]. They're hiring."

Union City was about an hour's drive from my home in Dobbs Ferry. A long ride, but I would chance it. I phoned Francis Oliver, the editor. He surprised me by almost putting me to work over the phone. I interviewed the next day and once again I was employed as a beat reporter. I took a pay cut, but regained my sanity.

Thus the changes continued.

The next night I attended the long anticipated wedding of Florence Rizzo. Her extravaganza lacked nothing. The fairy-tale festivities at the Enchanted Garden Hall filled the charged Bronx air with dance music, the smell of exotic foods and the sounds of 200 muffled voices.

I had to struggle through a thick crowd to work my way to one of the five bars that lined one side of the banquet hall. At the bridal party table I saw Florence and her husband surrounded by well-wishers, an array of white lilies, ushers, and the maid of honor. Her olive-tone face glowed as she appeared almost in a trance. I arrived late. The action was in full swing. I noticed the long waiting line to dance with the new bride. When she saw me, she waved and motioned me to get in line. Ten minutes later I was dancing with her against the background of music drowned out by the noisy crowd.

Florence looked remarkable with a stark white gown and a beautiful satin-trimmed hat. I move close to her and noticed dark circles under her eyes. Her makeup could not hide the stress her face revealed. She looked exhausted and her hands were damp with sweat.

"Finally I get a dance with the blushing bride," I said.

"Lucky you," she said and smiled.

"What an extravaganza." I said.

"Wake me up. It's like I am dreaming," she said. "I can't believe it."

"You deserve the best."

"I know I do," she answered.

The line of guests waiting to dance grew.

"My time is up," I said.

"Yes, it is."

I reached over and kissed her on the check.

"Eternal happiness."

"Eternal happiness," she replied.

"Time for a new life," I said.

"It already started at church this morning," she answered. Her voice possessed a sense of sincerity.

"I will always be happy for you, Flo."

I let go of her hand, and I felt an ominous feeling rush over me. My chest muscles tightened. I thought I was getting sick and started gasping for air.

I walked over to the bar and ordered a lime cooler with a double shot of vodka and gulped down a large mouthful. It felt good. I perked up and could breath again. I turned around and caught a glimpse of Jill with her family sitting around one of the scattered tables. She looked beautiful with long black curls and a dazzling pink floor-length gown. She didn't notice me and I made no attempt to go over to talk to her. It wasn't a good time. I had heard earlier that she was named city editor. I knew then why she pushed for me to quit the *Statesman*—less competition. I felt a little betrayed, but she deserved credit for her aggressiveness. She knew how get to the top. I let it go at that.

I finished my drink and walked across the dance floor to the exit and down the steel stares into the parking lot.

Driving toward the Saw Mill River Parkway, I could still hear the music coming from the wedding reception and as I moved farther away, it slowly faded to a dead silence.

Chapter 25
The *Hudson Dispatch*

Adversity has the effect of eliciting talents, which in
prosperous circumstances would have lain dormant.
—Horace

The *Hudson Dispatch* in Union City, New Jersey, a five-minute drive from Manhattan, employed three distinct types of journalists. One type was the nearly unemployable, broken-down newspaper drunk, another was the young dreamer who needed a training ground. In between the two were some rare, stabilized regulars who kept the paper on a somewhat sane course.

The newspaper, a few miles from the Weehawken banks where Aaron Burr killed Alexander Hamilton in a pistol duel, had been an enduring graveyard for over-the-hill journalists and a stopover for aspiring young writers waiting for another job.

"The *Dispatch* will hire any reporter with a pulse." That statement summed up the story.

"No one works here, they only pass through," a fellow journalist told me. "This is a place to brush up your resume and wait for another call. It's a wasteland for a career journalist."

During my stay at the *Dispatch* in the late 1960s, I discovered a rich, fertile mountain of talent that I brain-picked. I found a wealth of reporting wisdom from a crew that some called "a bunch of old drunks." They had more to offer a journalist than the most gifted Columbia School of Journalism professors. When they were sober, they were magnificent word masters and conscientious editors.

Copy Editor Frank Kerrigan* left a lasting impression me. He possessed the best writing, editing and reporting skills I ever encountered. I became his student. With his help, I wrote some of my best stories.

Kerrigan, a balding Irishman with white hair in keeping with his sixty-five earthly years, always wore a vest, white shirt, and tie. He dressed like a Wall Street executive. I wondered if his manner of dress gave him a feeling of past glory years or was perhaps to make him look taller. A former Army colonel, he claimed he worked with General Douglas MacArthur in writing his famous "Old Soldiers Never Die" speech. I listened with skepticism, but I listened.

"It was written on a paper napkin on a plane ride with General MacArthur," he said. MacArthur addressed Congress with his famous farewell speech after being fired by President Harry Truman.

Kerrigan hit the top as the chief public relations writer for Dole Pineapple until he drank himself of out of a job. A brilliant writing career went up in flames and his ashes sat across from me. He possessed credentials rarely seen in a journalist—a superb writer, editor, and reporter.

His dark side overwhelmed this once-bright "has-been." Frank came to work earlier every day and stopped next door at Mary's Bar, had a few draft beers, a can of sardines to absorb his beer breath, and a pack of crackers. He slipped out every few hours to do the same act, and returned to the newsroom giving off an unbearable stench. Somehow he lasted through the night.

Frank lived in Brooklyn, and without a car, getting home every night created a difficult chore. After work and brief drinking bouts, he hitched a ride to the subway, and by some miracle made it home.

One rainy, summer night, he broke his leg jumping from the subway platform onto the train. Breaking a leg and being alone at Frank's age is like a death sentence. Probably, he was ashamed to let his friends see the run-down apartment where he lived, so he discouraged company. When I left the newspaper, he was still home recuperating.

I lost a treasured article he edited for me. The story concerned a chemist getting fined for challenging the air pollution density in the Lincoln Tunnel. He took a nothing story and turned it into an interesting and enjoyable piece.

These writing minds at this insignificant newspaper amazed me; their fate saddened me.

The newspaper's editor, Francis (St. Francis) Oliver, an angel working as the editor, attended Mass every day, perhaps seeking strength to tend his troubled flock. Oliver, a trim-built son of Italian immigrants and another gray-haired staff member, started out as a copy boy, running for coffee, waiting on the editors and reporters. After years of reporting, he worked his way to the editorship position, a job few envied.

Oliver struck me as a warm, kind, corncob-pipe-smoking gentleman who showed few signs of carrying a heavy burden. His starched white shirt and stiff collar, and razor-edge creased pants gave him a military look.

"This will be the acid test for you. You are going to have the Union City and Weehawken beat," he'd said. "And if I like what I see, I'll give you a raise after three months."

I remained silent, just nodded my head and wondered if I'd be at the paper in three months.

He walked over to the water cooler and gulped down an aspirin with a cup of water. "I take one of these every day," he said." Keeps the heart in running order."

"I heard it thins the blood," I answered.

"You and I have something in common," he said, changing the subject.

"What?" I asked

"We are both Romans," he smiled.

"A New York and a New Jersey Roman." I looked at him intently. "That's a good combination."

I had little conversation with Oliver after that except for an occasional note praising some of my stories.

I saw him fly into a rage once. A headline on one of his editorials read, "Of Mices and Men."

It drew a roar and the headline writer sought other employment.

I worked Sundays and Oliver instructed me go to the area churches pick up the parish bulletins and find stories. The churches loved it, and it informed parishioners who slept in on Sunday.

I enjoyed covering Lincoln Tunnel traffic court where drivers were caught running through the tollbooths. Cheap drivers crashed the booth to escape paying fifty cents and ultimately paid a $120 fine; the height of stupidity.

There were amusing tales about some news staff catching the matinee Burlesque show across the street from the newspaper before coming to work and during cigarette breaks. I am told famous comedians like Bud Abbott and Lou Costello played at the Thirty Eighth Street Burlesque before moving on to New York City.

"Between the bumps and grinds of the girlie shows, the comedians kept 'em laughing and awake," recalled one of the old reporters.

A group of crusading ministers petitioned to padlock the show. The newspaper didn't endorse the move. Lack of paid attendance and an increase in porno shops finally forced the doors to shut. The shutdown saddened the day for working comedians and some of the news staff.

Hudson County had a reputation for corrupt politics. Federal indictments sent scores of politicians to jail. You needed a scorecard to keep track of the jailbirds.

The *Dispatch*, with a small staff, showed little interest in investigative reporting, a disappointing aspect of the newspaper. Like Kerrigan, the newspaper's glory years had gone the way of the Burlesque. If it ever won any editorial award, I wasn't unaware.

I did have a run-in with a reputed Mafia member. A fellow reporter suddenly died on the job, and I took over the beat. I rewrote one of his stories about a general contractor who managed a high-rise along the Hudson in North Bergen. It appeared to be a story with little merit until I received a phone call from an Anthony Russo*. He avoided his name in the newspaper like the plague.

"There are two things I dislike," he said in an angry tone. "My name in the newspaper and seeing the facts all wrong,"

"I am sorry," I said. "The paper will be happy to run a correction if something was wrong."

"No way," he shouted. "Just forget it."

"Whatever you want," I said, "Is there anything else?"

"Wait a minute," he said. "Your name sounds Italian. Are you?"

"That I am." I couldn't hold back a chuckle.

"What are doing writing for a rag newspaper," he said. "Can't you find a real job?"

"This is a real job," I said politely.

"Where do you live?" he asked.

"I can't discuss that," I said.

The line suddenly went dead.

Two days later I got a call at the main office in Union City. The caller didn't identify himself.

"And your name, sir?" I asked.

"Never mind," the voice said. "How would you like to take a bath in kerosene?"

I don't know if it was a threat or a joke. I knew about mob threats from Yonkers and the Bronx. The call, intended to frighten me, only raised my curiosity and amused me.

"No thanks, I prefer water," I said.

The phone went dead.

Chapter 26
A Mother's Tears

Work is love made visible. And if you cannot work with love but only with distaste, it is better that you should leave your work and sit at the gate of the temple and take alms from those who work with joy.
—Kahlil Gibran

I was back in the office after a few days off. I looked at my desk and gazed at the pile of work in front of me—rewrites, feature stuff, and government stuff. It was at that moment I received a phone call from a distraught mother.

"You ran a story of my son in his football uniform, talked about how bad he was, and never mentioned what a great football star he was," she sobbed.

I listened.

"Couldn't you write something nice about my son?" Her sobs had subsided, but her voice was shaky. "He died alone in the street. Isn't that punishment enough? Your paper had to take him over the coals. Where is the respect and dignity?"

I wanted to tell her that it was probably the only photo we had of her son, and we weren't a public relations firm. We just reported the news. I did, however, relate to her sorrow.

"I can't promise you anything, but let me take a look at the story."

His death had happened on a steaming July night in 1969; one day after the Apollo 11 astronauts walked on the moon. Eighteen-year-old Joe Hoffer* was found dead on the streets of Union City. The

141

high school football star died of a drug overdose. America's drug abuse numbers ran out of control during the Vietnam War years.

The *Dispatch* ran a short story and photo of Hoffer wearing his football uniform. The newspaper needed most of its space for the moon landing events. I gave the story a quick read.

"Hoffer was just another stupid 'coke head' who didn't take any advice, and he paid for it," a reporter said.

No. His mother paid for it. Drug users, considered the scum of the earth, received little sympathy. These addicted creatures were blamed for a rise in crime, despicable neighborhoods and the changed face of America. Hoffer, a habitual heroin user, qualified as one of the losers.

"Rehabilitation is a joke," a police official said. "All you do is sober them up so they can hit the streets again."

Hoffer's death happened on my regular beat during the days I had off. In the New York City metropolitan area, newsrooms got almost a murder a day. The tragic events poured in and along with war news, one more drug death was no big deal. You grew another layer of skin and became immune to the tragedy around you. Like a soldier in a combat zone, you live with it. With Hoffer, few grieved and after a few days, he became an insignificant memory. Life must go on.

Criticism ran high with newspaper stories, and most papers attempted to correct mistakes, but Hoffer's mother targeted fairness. Information gathering should not be opinionated. Write the stories. I heard a saying somewhere, "Without offense to friend or foe, we sketch your world exactly as it goes."

A tug pulled at my heart, though. I looked again at the work-covered desk. How am I going to get through this and find time to write a story on Hoffer? Stories run cold quickly. Few news stories hold lasting interest; most get stale overnight.

I took a closer look at the story. With an audible sigh, I picked up the phone and called his school to dig up some old sports stories about this football star. "Joe was blessed. This football star had it all. He was young, handsome, and a superb athlete. His season is over, at least here on earth."

I worked up what I hoped was a feature that would bring a bit of solace to Joe's mother. The story highlighted Joe Hoffer's glory years in high school.

The second phone call from his mother came the minute the newspaper hit the street that night. She was still crying, but this time, they were tears of joy.

"Finally someone discovered something good to say about my son," she said.

"It was easy to find."

Editor Oliver sent me a pleasant note about how much he admired the piece. I wished I could have looked into that mother's face as she read about her son. I never heard from her again, but I felt good about the story and remembered a part of Gibran's quote, *Work is love made visible.*

Chapter 27
Hoboken:
No Jewel on the Hudson

Hoboken, New Jersey, home of Frank Sinatra, was no jewel on the Hudson in the late '60s. It was a dilapidated, crime-ridden city in transition. Italians and Irish moved to the suburbs. Hoboken remained in urban limbo, with little employment and little hope, until the late '80s when developers realized this waterfront community was a diamond in the rough.

Today, waterfront luxury condos that line the Hudson River cost from five hundred thousands dollars to a few million. This once almost forgotten town, fifteen minutes to Manhattan by the Weehawken Ferry, is now a hot spot for singles and young New York executives on the move. Mass development created a dream community, loaded with lively nightclubs and gourmet restaurants. It's a far cry from the Hoboken I left in the late '60s.

The extent of my luxury in dreary Hoboken consisted of a closet-size pressroom a few yards from the rundown police station near Washington Street. Once night fell, the city appeared abandoned.

Every night the small radio on my desk pumped out "Strangers in the Night," Sinatra's big hit then. It was a high time for "Ol' Blue Eyes," but a low point for his hometown. The newspapers advertised waterfront properties at bargain basement prices. Any noise that rang out from the city came from the Hoboken police station.

A strange twist of events happened on a chilly October night when I heard cops arguing in the room next to me. I tried to shut out the voices and focus on the work, but the loud, boisterous voices drowned out my concentration. Two cops almost came to blows over goods from an overturned railroad car. Hundreds of cans filled with coffee had spilled out. The accident occurred earlier in the day and the coffee cans lined a railroad spur not far from the police station. One policeman thought it was open season on the coffee.

"Oh, it's free to take. Once the car overturned, the coffee becomes unusable, and it's up for grabs. The insurance company just leaves them to be carted away."

I chuckled. *Yeah, I bet.*

A fellow reporter smiled, remarking that some cops in north Jersey think every day is Christmas. "They're always looking a gift, not a bribe, but a gift." Somehow the argument was settled and the cans of coffee found a home. A funny story, yes, but the tale is only a bite out of the police corruption that ran almost uncontrollable in New Jersey and New York in the topsy-turvy '60s.

Shaking down drug dealers, the biggest game in police circles, proved to be the downfall of crooked cops. Cops tabbed drug dealers as easy pickings. Who are the dealers going to tell? No one believed scum drug dealers, until undercover New York City policeman Frank Serpico surfaced and exposed one the biggest police scandals in the area's history. The scandal sent cops to prison. Al Pacino starred in a movie, *Serpico*, about the disgrace.

The Hoboken pressroom and the jail were throwbacks to the Wild West. On any night you might hear wailing and banging on the walls of the jail. I never saw police brutality, but the obscene dialogue exchanged by the police and inmates was enough to drive one insane. I ranked it as the wildest, noisiest, and most disoriented place to work for even the most patient journalist.

When the regular Hoboken reporter returned from vacation, I hurried over to shake his hand tightly and not let him go. I wanted to hug the reporter with joy. "What a pleasure to have you back."

He looked at me and smiled. "Was it that bad?"

"Worse," I said.

Editor Francis Oliver never sent me to Hoboken again. He must have been psychic.

A few days later, Oliver did call me into his office. With a somber face, he asked me to write on story on a young Catholic priest who left to the church to marry his personal secretary. An emotional blow to a deeply religious man, the story made Oliver uncomfortable. It touched home base. In the late '60s, some priests were making a mad rush out the door to do other things with their lives.

The priesthood started changing and never would be the same again. As the years went by, large-scale sex scandals never imagined in history rocked the Catholic Church.

When I interviewed the priest, he seemed content about his decision. "Ruth and I love each other, and we will find another way to serve God."

He justified breaking his vows as an act of love. Some of the church members were shocked, but most took it in stride.

"Priests should be able to get married," said one church member.

Oliver, a strong conservative Catholic, opposed any change in the church policy, but remained silent about the issue in his editorials. Like most Catholics, Oliver hoped the church dust would settle and return to normal. Little did he or the world know that it was the beginning of a chain of events that would rock the Catholic Church to the doorstep of inconceivable shame.

Chapter 28
Friends You Leave Behind

Friendship is the hardest thing in the world to explain. It's not something you learn in school. But if you haven't learned the meaning of friendship, you really haven't learned anything.
—Mohammed Ali

The *Dispatch* left me with a deep sense of gratitude for my few close friends. When I departed, good friends stayed behind, many forever. The empty feeling of not seeing them again remained deep-seated within me for several years. However, two reporters, Ray Bourdious and Tom Incantalupo, became lifelong friends.

Bourdious, a journeyman journalist, World War II pilot, and a product of City College of New York, worked the *Dispatch* copy desk in between interviewing for other jobs. As though obsessed, Ray never stopped sending out resumes.

Fifty years old, of medium height with black hair, this Bronx native loved the "good life." He had traveled the world. Ray spoke fluent French, lived in Paris for a few years and married an Italian-born beauty. Catherine stayed home while Ray toured the world. In spite of his incessant wanderings, his marriage remained strong and harmonious. Restless, Ray could not stay in one job more than a year.

"As soon as I get a big editor's job in New York, I'll call for you," he joked.

Ray and I had a lot in common. We never wanted to go home after work. The two of us would hit the nightclubs in New York and visit

147

places that celebrities patronized. Ray liked to go to a restaurant in Manhattan where Johnny Carson, based in New York in that era, sat at the bar and drank. One night Ray walked up next to Carson, who was surrounded by friends, and said hello. Carson didn't seem to mind.

Paying for parking under any condition was taboo to Ray. He would spend hours looking for free parking. He lived in Queens, parked in the street, and took pride in finding an available parking space. He lived in a rent-controlled apartment for $140 a month for twenty years. Ray kept the apartment even after he moved to Washington to take a job with the *Seafarers' Union* publication.

Ray would play an important part in my career. He helped me get a fill-in copy editor job at the New York *Daily News*. Later he was instrumental in my being hired for a copy editor's job at the *Newark Evening News*, one the best newspapers in the metropolitan area.

Tom Incantalupo, a 22-year-old Brooklynite, worked the Secaucus beat near the garbage disposal center. Later it became the famous Meadowlands sports complex. Tom, a son of an Italian New York City sanitation worker, graduated from the City College of New York. He started his first reporting job at the *Dispatch*.

A hard working reporter, Tom seemed to have no bad habits. A talkative bundle of energy, Tom walked with a limp from a childhood hip operation. He drank little and appeared to be an ideal "catch," but he had trouble finding a date. His shyness, limp, and thick glasses made it difficult for him to connect with women.

At a New York party, I introduced Tom to a Colombian woman I knew from Yonkers. Behind his large glasses, he turned starry-eyed, and it was instant love for Betty, a tiny blonde salesperson.

After a short relationship, Tom wanted to take her home to meet his father and mother. "I don't know how they are going to take the fact that I am dating a Colombian woman." He took off his oversized eyeglasses, then replaced them. "I probably would never find the right Italian woman."

Tom's parents did buck the relationship for a time, and then gave in. I attended their wedding at the Village on the Green in Manhattan.

Tom later got a job with *Newsday* as the automobile writer.

I visited his home in Long Island once in the early '80s. Later I lost track of him and we didn't keep in touch.

For several months I stayed at the *Dispatch*, and also worked for a time at a weekly paper, the *North Bergen Record*. One day, out of the blue, Ray called me. "There's an opening at the *Newark Evening News*. Give Chief Copy Editor Stan King a call. I'm sure he'll hire you."

Ray was right. Three weeks later I started working for the *Newark Evening News*.

Saying goodbye to the *Dispatch* didn't take long. I would see Tom and Ray again.

As far as the rest of staff, we were hardly acquaintances. My farewell to Editor Oliver took less than a minute. I admired the man, not as a brilliant editor, but as a perfect gentleman.

"You did a remarkable job," Oliver said to me, then bit on his pipe. He looked at me. I gazed back at him sitting in his office chair. I thought he must have repeated those words a hundred times before to reporters passing through the door. He sounded sincere.

"If you ever need a job, don't hesitate to phone me," he said.

"Thanks, Francis. I won't. I enjoyed working for you." I paused. "And hey, you never know. If I ever need a job again, I'll certainly call you."

"You are going to the best paper in New Jersey," he said. "The *Newark News* doesn't hire just anyone." He ended his remarks with a smile.

Not like here, I thought. I shook his hand, walked out, and waved goodbye to the unaware, uncaring news staff.

There were no going-away parties. One quick look back at the old dimly-lit newsroom was my farewell. I thought of Frank Kerrigan, who still nursed a broken leg at home. I wondered if I'd ever see him again.

I hurried next door to Mary's bar, downed a draft beer, and minutes later I disappeared into the Lincoln Tunnel.

Chapter 29
The Little *New York Times*

Pick battles big enough to matter,
small enough to win.
                    —Jonathan Kozol

Driving to work at the *Newark Evening News,* I looked around me. The area reminded me of a movie I saw about Berlin after World War II. Newark, too, looked like a bombed out city. The national race riots of 1967 left devastation. During one of the worst riots in this country's history, sixty people were killed here, including a policeman.

A local civil war broke out. Buildings were burned to the ground. Looters struck everywhere and lawlessness prevailed. In the middle of this torn city were big businesses like Prudential, a symbol of Newark, attempting to put the pieces back together.

"A city without hope," one reporter said. "It's spiritually dead and will never come back. Never will Newark rank with the great cities of this country again."

"They should level it and start all over," another reporter said.

A scary place saturated with crime, drugs, and political corruption, Newark appeared to be on life support. This once industrial giant, where Thomas Edison first worked on the light bulb before moving his labratory to Menlo Park, was a shell of its glorious past.

The appalling conditions convinced me to continue to live in Dobbs Ferry. I commuted eighty miles a day. The riots were gone, but a combat zone atmosphere remained.

The newspaper, centered in the heart of Newark on Market Street, was an extremely dangerous place to work nights at that time. It got so bad that women were not allowed to work after five o'clock in the afternoon. Since we were paid in cash, payday proved to be the riskiest time for *Newark News* employees. Muggers had an array of prey to pick from. No one understood the incomprehensible decision by management to pay employees in cash.

Lack of parking heightened the problems. Employees had no choice but to park in the street. That ignited trouble. If you work in a dangerous part of any city and do the same thing every day, an attentive thief is going to take advantage of that repetition. Cars left unattended during work shifts were stolen. The bad guys knew every move news employees made. My car, broken into several times, made the stolen list my second month on the job. I never recovered it. It probably wound up in some chop shop.

The former owners of the *Newark News*, the Scudder family, wanted to stay downtown and put a positive spin on the crumbling area. The questionable choice did nothing to help Newark's infamous reputation. It only hurt the workers and the newspaper.

Like glue, unfavorable credentials stuck firmly to the city until the late '80s when the "New Newark" emerged from the ashes of the riots. The city, although not out of the woods, showed signs of life as new buildings were built and economic health returned.

Years before, the Scudder family made the Newark News one of the best newspapers in New Jersey. The paper covered the state and had reporters or branches in New York, the United Nations, Trenton, Washington and Saigon. It peaked in the early '60s and dipped after the riots.

When I arrived in the late '60s, the Scudders had recently sold the newspaper to Media General, a newspaper chain out of Virginia. Media General owned the *Tampa Tribune* and some small newspapers. The company, not interested in the Newark paper, wanted the profit-making Garden State Paper Company. The Scudders were smart enough to put the *Newark News* into the package with the newsprint firm—no *Newark News*, no Garden State Paper Company.

Reluctantly, Media General purchased both, with secret plans to cut the newspaper down to what was called a "profitable size." Instead of attempting to sell the Newark paper, Media General attempted to squeeze profit out it.

I worked on the newspaper's universal desk, which edited wire stories from around the world. I could write headlines about the Vietnam War, the Middle East and the Charles Manson murders in my sleep.

Eight copy editors and Chief Copy Editor Stanley King worked at a torrid pace, pumping state, national, and world news into the paper. King, a caring boss, had his idiosyncrasies. He strongly believed that he should never get too friendly with the staff, so he lunched by himself every day.

The paper had some of the best copy editors in the business. I felt like an amateur among the geniuses. A great number of these news people went to work for the *New York Times* and other prestigious papers. Some editors called it "The little *New York Times*."

The competition, the *Newark Star Ledger*, owned by the Newhouse chain, did little to take the lead over the *Newark News* until Media General's stupid decision to revamp the newspaper.

In the early '70s, after working in Newark for about a year, King slipped out the news that Media General planned a big cut in the staff. Unrest and fear swept over the newsroom.

Jane Tate*, a pipe-smoking, brilliant copy editor, was the first to alert me that a change was in the works. "Media General is going to ruin this paper," she said. "There's talk of a union."

I couldn't stop the disturbed feeling that took over. "I'm all ears. Tell me what you know."

"There is a secret plan to melt down 40 percent of the staff," she said. "They never wanted this newspaper in the first place," she added.

"The greedy Scudder family owed it to the employees to find a caring owner," she said. "A huge cut in the staff will slice the quality out of this paper."

I listened and nodded my head while she described the nightmare that lay ahead for the employees.

One night, a group of workers broke into the publisher's office, obtained the plans, reprinted them, and distributed the bad news to some of the 900 employees. The list had names and departments ready to be axed. Turmoil erupted in the newsroom, with a cry for a hasty union organization.

Media General leaked the word out by company sympathizers that a union would destroy the newspaper. The warning was brushed off as a scare tactic.

Union organizers weren't sure of where I stood, and knew the action could have serious consequences. It may not be legal, but companies find a way to push the union supporters out the door.

Later, one of the copy editors, Joe Mack*, called me on an office phone. "I need to talk to you."

"About what?"

"About a union," he said. "A bunch of employees are getting together at the Pen and Pencil for a drink and we would like to invite you."

"Fine," I said. No harm in listening. I made my plans to go.

At the restaurant, one of the organizers wanted to know where I stood as far as the union was concerned.

"I would support anything that would save jobs."

"Did you know that Media General is about to ax half the staff?"

"I heard about it."

"Did you know you might be one who will still have a job?"

"I don't know anything," I said.

"Would you vote for a union?"

"I might." At that instant I became a trusted friend of the union organizers.

In a matter of days the union campaign picked up steam. A union victory seemed certain. In spite of the gigantic momentum, there remained a vacuum, a lack of the confidence, that voting in a union would be enough to save jobs. An ominous feeling came over me as

I faced the obscure future.

I felt uncomfortable leaving my fate to others. Not being the captain of my own ship, I would have to depend on the union to take me through the rough waters. But there were few choices. We could concede to the company's demand and throw half the staff to the lions, and wait for Media General to get rid of the rest of us later, or fight to save the jobs now.

The following Monday, the nightmare emerged as the general manager, Bruce Mair, a former *Philadelphia Inquirer* publisher, called a general meeting of the newspaper's employees.

He broke the bad news.

Chapter 30
A Union, a Strike,
and the Picket Line

News executive Bruce Mair's voice roared across the crowded *Newark News* newsroom.

He wanted to make sure the employees heard him. James Idema, executive editor, stood motionless in the rear of the room. Publisher Richard B. Scudder was absent.

"Media General has made a painful decision to cut the *Newark News* staff about 40 percent." Mair said.

"It's a somber time, especially for those who have given twenty and thirty years of dedicated service to this paper. But it's trim to the bone or close the door.

"When we purchased the newspaper a few years ago, we knew it would be a challenge to make it a profitable venture. Our first step is to cut costs, and people are the most expensive of those costs."

He stopped, took a deep breath, and reached for the glass of ice water on the table as the quiet news staff looked on and listened intensely.

"I know that some of you want to organize a union," he said. "I understand a vote is scheduled." He hesitated and a gazed directly at one of the organizers. "That would be the kiss of death," he said. "A union here would be the final nail in this troubled newspaper's coffin.

"If we cut costs now, we can save some jobs and the newspaper. If we are forced to do something else, we may lose it all," he said.

"Think about it. Think about the other newspapers in the

metropolitan area that have gone to the graveyard because of union demands, the prestigious *Journal American* for one, and the *New York Herald Tribune* for another," he added.

"As soon as the list of laid off employees is computed, they will be posted," he said. "I don't think it's appropriate to take any questions right know."

With that, he walked out of a dead silent newsroom.

The tough speech signaled Media General's aggressive policy. They were going to cut the staff at any cost.

In February 1971, union organizers called for a strike vote after a newly organized union had been voted in.

When Media General heard the disappointing results, it dug in its heels, played hardball, and decided not to even talk to the union. It was a devastating blow for Media General. Now it would be difficult even to sell the newspaper.

After failing to schedule talks with the company, the union gave an ultimatum: sit for talks or we walk the picket line. Media General remained tough and refused to even recognize the union. Dark clouds appeared over Market Street as a strike loomed over the horizon.

At the same time, I was scheduled to have a leg operation in Bronx Kingsbridge Hospital. The injury resulted from an Army parachute jump in Fort Campbell, Kentucky. I put off the operation for years until the pain became unbearable.

Going to Kingsbridge, a dilapidated Veterans Hospital, during the Vietnam War was a living nightmare. The ancient hospital, loaded with drug dealers, drunks, and crawling roaches, needed a major facelift. It was a forgotten institution where wounded Vietnam veterans were sent to be treated, convalesce, or die.

Given a bed in an empty ward, I couldn't believe what I saw. Wallpaper and paint were peeling off the walls and falling to the floor. The toilets and washrooms were filthy, deplorable by any health standards. I saw wounded vets limping around the hallways looking for drugs and booze. Hospital personnel were overloaded and uncaring. After a week of prep work, I had my operation by a surgeon fresh out of medical school. As sore as I was, I wanted out.

I pushed the doctors for an early discharge for my mental health.

One of the of saddest moments of my stay occurred when I took the elevator to the wrong floor and walked into a ward that had paralyzed and basket-case veterans, no arms and no legs, just torsos. I left in tears. I prayed that they were well taken care of. I complained to hospital officials about other conditions, but no one seemed concerned. Public officials were aware, but stalled in doing anything. The news about Kingsbridge was widely known, but little was done to correct the problems. Veterans hospitals then were not noted for being the best healthcare facilities, but Kingsbridge ranked with the worst.

Years later, *Life* magazine did an expose on the hospital. Since then, a new, clean, modern facility has been built. Ironically, a lifetime friend of mine, William Fote, a former Park Bench Gang friend of mine who was a former government construction engineer, played a key role in building the new hospital.

Returning to the *Newark News* after a four-week medical leave, trouble brewed and a strike appeared imminent.

The union officials held an emergency meeting and set a strike deadline.

"It's time for action," the leader said. "The pleading is over, the real battle is about to start.

"We're going to shut the newspaper down until the company comes to the table," he said.

A strike vote early in May 1971 set the stage for immediate picket lines that dotted Newark's Market Street. After ninety years of operation, the *Newark News* presses stopped. Media General, still hoping to keep the newspaper going and kill off the union, decided to appeal to editorial employees, who were hard-pressed for money, to cross the picket line.

"Employees are urged to come to work. We are going to try to get a newspaper out," urged management.

With most of workers strapped with families to feed and mortgages, the offer sounded inviting. And with no unemployment insurance available because of a strike, a few employees caved in and walked by their fellow workers on the picket line.

"I got a family to feed, and I have a house to pay for, and I have children in college," a striker cried out in the union meeting. "I can't afford to stay out of work more than a week," he said. "I'm sorry, but I'm going to cross the picket line. And God help anyone who tries to stop me."

Good friends became bitter enemies.

"All of us are in the same boat," said the officer. "The company wants to split us and then break us. If we stick together, we get what we want."

The union rallies helped morale a little. Celebrities came in to support the paper. The television stations carried news about the strike for a couple of weeks and then things started to sputter. With the company still adamant, the union fire slowly faded to bewilderment. Strikers were beginning to think it was hopeless.

Media General smelled death in the air and made plans to sell the rich *Sunday Newark News* circulation and its modern presses to the competitor, the *Newark Star Ledger*. If the management couldn't sell the newspaper, it would dismantle it.

I continued walking the picket line for five months, and did some part-time and free-lance work in New York.

The strike dragged on for more than a year and became one of the longest newspaper strikes in the country's history. Many believed the newspaper might never publish again.

When talks finally got under way and the strike settled in April 1972, the newspaper had lost its loyal readers, most of the top staff, and its credentials. With little left, the *Newark News* hobbled along for a few more months before collapsing.

To many of the remaining workers, the disastrous strike cost them their homes and their families. Some were forced into bankruptcy. I barely kept it together with part-time jobs, my wife working, and my dad's help. Although it was a financial low for me, I never regretted it. The strike became a moral issue; there needed to be a sense of dignity against supporting an unjust action by Media General. The company had little respect for *Newark News* employees and less for the integrity of the newspaper.

The *News* attempted, hopelessly, to circulate a five-day-a-week paper and fell on its face. The *Newark News* ceased publication on August 31, 1972, no surprise to anyone.

Although the union took some of the blame for the death of the Newark News, it was clear that Media General stood out as the major culprit.

The desire to run a first-class newspaper was not in Media General's plans. It only wanted the Garden State Paper Company, not the newspaper. Media General looked at the *Newark News* as a losing proposition, never giving it a chance. It was a monkey on its back that it finally shook loose. The Scudder family, who cared less about their loyal employees and more about money, never looked for a buyer who had some interest in the newspaper. The Scudder family left 900 employees, like abandoned children, at the doorstep of an uncaring Media General.

And so "The Gray Lady on Market Street," the Pulitzer Prize winning newspaper, vanished.

This now ghost of New Jersey's past had a rich legacy. It produced prominent writers like Howard Grais, who created the Uncle Wiggly characters.

Lillian McNamara launched the Bobbsey Twins series.

Richard Reeves became a national columnist and wrote best-selling books including *President Kennedy: Profile of Power*.

Arthur Sylvester, a Kennedy aide, became Assistant Secretary of Defense for Public Affairs.

George Oslin invented the singing telegram.

John Cunningham was a New Jersey historian.

Willie Ratner was a boxing writer.

Joe Katz was press secretary for New Jersey Governor Richard Hughes.

I never returned to work at the *News* after the strike settled in April 1972. After six months of living at the poverty level and walking the picket lines, I started interviewing for other jobs.

I thought about Stan King, who was almost in tears as he

addressed the copy editors the day we walked out.

"This is the end for the Newark News. I'll probably never work with some of you people again," he said. I never saw Stan again.

One bright August day in 1971, I received a call from a Charles Meredith III, a publisher of a small Bucks County, Pennsylvania, newspaper. He wanted a tough, experienced editor to inject new life into a dying, small daily newspaper. I had sent him a resume and he replied. He wanted to me to come to Quakertown, a small Pennsylvania Dutch community in upper Bucks County, 75 miles from Manhattan.

"You're in for one, long, beautiful ride in the country," said one acquaintance. I never imagined how long.

Chapter 31
Bucks County, Pennsylvania

Every beginning is a consequence—every beginning
ends something.

—Paul Valery

Historians love Buck County, Pennsylvania. A few miles from Philadelphia and seventy-five miles form New York City, the beautiful rolling hills and fertile farmland have the ghosts of James A. Michener and Pearl S. Buck strolling around this gorgeous piece of real estate. There is so much rich American history in the county, dating back to William Penn and George Washington, who crossed the Delaware from Bucks County. One would need an encyclopedia to list everything. I found the pastoral land fascinating.

I had an appointment with Charles Meredith III, publisher and owner of the *Free Press*, a small daily newspaper in upper Bucks. The one-hundred-year-old newspaper in the heart of Quakertown was not far from where the Revolutionary army hid the Liberty Bell from the British in the autumn of 1777 before taking the bell to Allentown.

A small built, light blond man, he was a dead ringer for television commentator Dick Cavett. Meredith explained to me he was departing from his Republican County Commissioner post to devote his time to running the newspaper along with his mother Ella. His father, Charles Meredith II, died a few years earlier, leaving the financially strapped newspaper to his University of Pennsylvania graduate son, to resurrect it from the death bed.

"I need an experienced editor who can do it all," he said as he toyed with his bow tie, his trademark. We talked in his tiny, overheated office a few feet from the rumbling press, which at times drowned out our voices. The newsroom looked like a modern version of the "Tombstone Epitaph" that you see in cowboy movies.

"I know your big city news experience will help, and I know you can run a newsroom, but this is a hands-on job, which gets right into the community. They want to come in and talk to the editor any time of the day," he said.

"I don't think I will have any trouble with that," I said. "I've lived in a small city for part of my life and understand the small-community thinking," I said. "People are pretty much the same, wherever you go."

He nodded his head and continued to look at my resume.

"I see you were an Army paratrooper," he said. "I like military people. I am a proud member of the Pennsylvanian First, a military unit going back to the Revolutionary War." He smiled and continued.

"I've received a lot of resumes for this job, and I'm going to make my decision soon."

"The sooner, the better," I said. "I know you want to make sure you get the right editor. There is a lot of work to do here, and it won't be easy, even for the most experienced editor," I said.

Meredith, aware of the mammoth task, knew the newspaper's life was on the line.

The *Free Press*, sandwiched between two big newspapers, the *Philadelphia Inquirer* and the *Morning Call* in Allentown, made it an incredibly tough, competitive area.

"My grandfather, the first Charles Meredith, founded the *Free Press* as a weekly. Very profitable. The decision to go daily took us on a different road and a very expensive one. We had to add to the staff and put on more production costs. We had to satisfy the advertisers or be swallowed up by the competitors.

"At times I wonder if we made the right decision," he said and shifted the conversation.

"My grandfather was a sheriff before becoming a publisher, and the last criminal to be hanged in the county was under my grandfather's tenure," he said with a smile.

"Well, he didn't oppose the death penalty," I said with a wide grin.

We got down to the last and more serious part of the interview—money.

"What kind of money are you looking for?" he said

"What are you paying?" I asked.

"One hundred and eighty five dollars a week, health benefits, and a great community to work in and raise a family," he said. A little low, but I knew I couldn't jack it up. I had to prove myself first. I made twice that in Newark. But I knew this wasn't Newark.

"Sounds like the place I would like to work," I said.

"Good," he said. "That will narrow my choices down."

I hesitated, then decided to talk about the future.

"I'm going to have to clear the air on a few other things," I said. "If you hire me, I want to make sure this is not one of those jobs where in a few weeks you change your mind and editors."

He understood.

"It would be on a probationary period, and then I would want you to live here and raise your family and retire with the newspaper."

That's what I wanted to hear.

He shook my hand and sounded sincere.

"I'll let you know my decision in a few weeks," he said as we both walked toward the door.

"I enjoyed the visit and the interesting interview," I said. "And especially talking about your grandfather. He would have made a fascinating story." I added, "You're right, it's a beautiful area to raise a family.

"I'll wait to hear from you," I said as I walked down the outside steps, passing by the two huge white pillars of the building.

I walked to my car, noticed my meter was red, but no parking ticket, just a hospitable reminder on the windshield.

"My kind of town," I thought as I headed back to New York to wait for a decision.

Chapter 32
Yonkers Revisited

No servitude is more disgraceful than that which is self-imposed.

—Seneca

In between pounding the pavement on the picket line in Newark and waiting for the Bucks County decision, I received a disturbing call from Bill Blair from the *Yonkers Herald Statesman*.

"I'm in serious trouble," he said early on an August Monday morning.

"What can I do to help?" I said.

"I got this woman pregnant," he said without going into details.

"Who, Jill?" I said.

"No, no, this Spanish chick I've been dating," he said.

"Who the hell is she?" I said, since I hadn't seen him or any of the *Yonkers* staffers in months.

"Let's have some coffee and I'll explain it to you," he said.

"I'll meet you at Sam's in Dobbs," I said.

"What was that all about?" my wife said as I started getting dressed and headed out the door.

"A friend of mine is in a little trouble," I said, downplaying the ordeal. "Nothing serious," I said as I walked down the stairs of the apartment into the car and headed for Sam's.

Bill got there before I arrived and was smoking a king-size cigarette, a habit that bothered me since my lung operation.

I walked in, sat down, and immediately complained.

"Bill, if we're going to talk for a while, you got to stop smoking, at least until I leave," I said.

"Okay, okay," he nervously replied. "I apologize."

The waitress brought me a hot cup of coffee and I took a sip.

"Okay, Bill, start from the beginning," I said.

"Well, about three months ago, I was in the Casa D'Roma and this gorgeous Spanish girl comes in. I mean a real beauty," he said. "She has jet black, long hair, black eyes, slim, and was wearing a well-cut white summer suit," he said.

"She is with a young Spanish guy, and they sit next to me at the bar," he said.

"I strike up a conversation with the couple, and before you know it, we are getting smashed and having a ball. When the guy goes to the restroom, the girl gets really friendly. One word led to another, and I asked her out. She barely understands English, but got my message quite clear. She says the guy with her is just a friend and she accepted my invitation to dinner."

He hesitated a moment, reached for a cigarette, and put it in his mouth, but didn't light it.

"You're hearing the beginning of a wild love affair. We did everything together. We dined in Manhattan every night, danced in the cafes in the Village, drank the best wine, and went to the weekend bed-and-breakfasts in the Catskills.

"The breezy rides along the Hudson River to West Point made me feel alive again. We were almost inseparable. She is a gorgeous, soft, sweet loving doll. It was such a refreshing time in my life," he continued.

"About three weeks ago, she comes to me in tears and tells me she is going to have my baby. I was shocked. I thought she was taking the pill. All sorts of things are racing through my mind. I even ask her if she had been sleeping with another guy. For some crazy reason, I'm just like all men who first cry out, 'It's not mine.'

"She said, 'No never, only you. How could you even think that?'

"I asked her if she wanted to have the baby. She says only if I marry her."

"I am sure you forgot to tell her you already had a wife," I said.

"I would love to have the baby, but not at the price of bigamy. And no way I'm going to divorce my wife," he said.

"I don't know what to tell you," I said.

"She says if I don't marry her, she going to have an abortion."

"That's stupid," I said. "Bill, you know abortion is illegal, and her only choice is the butchers." I said. It was 1971.

"That's the reason I wanted to talk to you. I know there was a story about an abortion doctor on North Broadway, and I wonder if that is the way to go.

"Are you nuts?" I said. "What the hell is the matter with you? Those lousy doctors will ruin her insides. She's just a kid," I said angrily. "And there is no sane reason not to have the baby," I added.

"You better talk to her about having the baby and at least giving it up for adoption," I said. "There are millions of childless couples who want children. Bill, you and your wife are one of the childless couples."

"Can you imagine me bringing home the kid to my wife?" he answered.

"Why not?" I replied. He didn't want to hear any more about that and shifted the conversation.

"She already went to one doctor, and he has been giving her shots to bring on her period and nothing happened."

"You are making me sick," I said.

"Let me give you my advice. Don't let the butchers at her. Let her have the baby. Talk to her," I said.

"Okay, okay, I am going to talk to her this week," Bill said as we finished our coffee and walked out the door.

"Hey, that reminds me, what happened to Jill? Are you still seeing her?" I asked.

"I knew you would ask," he said with a smile. "No, we broke it off. She got promoted to the city editor's job and now she wants to lead a normal married life, so she says. She is getting a little tired of going to bed with me on Saturday mornings, in between going shopping," he remarked. "That is the only time we see each other anymore. You know what's strange about it?" he said with a smile. "You can't even trust your wife to go shopping on Saturday morning without her cheating on you."

"Oh, how about your wife?" Remember her? You do have a wife?"

"She's about ready to unload me," Bill said.

"I wonder why," I said.

"I know this is hard to believe, but I do want to save my marriage," he said.

"If I don't get out of this area and settle down, she's finished with me. Now I got these other problems facing me," he said.

"You have a lot of work ahead of you," I said. "You played, Bill, and now it's time to pay the piper. No free lunches, not even in bed," I said.

We shook hands in front of the diner.

"Keep in touch," I said.

He hesitated before getting in his car. "I need your help," he said. "You're the only guy I can talk to about these things."

"I think you're going to need more than my help," I said.

"Like who?" He smiled.

"Like a miracle man or the Pope," I said, smiling back and getting into my car to head home.

That son of a bitch is facing some rough weather, I thought. He's going to blow it all.

Later that the morning, I got another phone call.

It was Charles Meredith III.

The Bucks County publisher wanted me to come to his home for a second interview. I would accept the job at that interview.

The morning sun broke through the clouds and came shining in through the windowpane on my face. I felt a warm, comfortable glow.

It was the beginning of a wonderful day.

Chapter 33
Visiting the Center of Paradise

Today a new sun rises; everything is animated,
everything speaks to me of my passion,
everything invites me to cherish.
　　　　　—Anne de Lenclos

Quakertown, Pennsylvania! Here we were, my family and I, once again starting a new life. We sat with the family of Charles Meredith III in the living room of their large white Victorian house on Juniper Street. A couple of weeks later, I would take over the editor's position for the *Free Press*. At Meredith's invitation, we were checking out our families' compatibility.

"You will enjoy being a part of the *Free Press's* family," Meredith said. Charles loved to use the word *family*, especially when speaking to employees—a good corporate tool, but I thought a bit plastic.

"This is a great place to raise a family and hopefully retire." He praised the area as though describing the center of paradise. He traveled often and had attended the University of Pennsylvania in nearby Philadelphia, but he spent most of his life in upper Bucks County.

Meredith had recently terminated his political life as county commissioner. With his mother pushing, he decided to take the reigns of the distressed newspaper. Charles knew he needed a lot of help, the right help. He was neither a polished statesman nor an experienced publisher, but he had no place to go except to try to keep the financially troubled newspaper alive. He would rely on a superior advertising director and an attractive news package to turn the financial picture around.

I was excited about my new position, but I had almost turned it down. The challenge intrigued me, however, and it truly was a paradise in which to raise a family.

His wife, Elizabeth, daughter of a physician, appeared to be cultured and charming. The young children, Charles IV, Anne, and Catherine, were pleasant and polite. It seemed a little unusual, though, to sit inside on a hot August afternoon and drink hot coffee with no food or snacks. I was puzzled by the skimpy hospitality, but shrugged it off.

As we were preparing to leave, the children started some ghastly boasting that caught me off guard. I couldn't believe the torrent of words that poured from such youngsters. Anne and Charles IV, almost together as in a race, dashed over to a beautiful China closet and a dresser right next to it.

"This is my inheritance," said five-year-old Anne as she pointed to the China cabinet. "It will be mine when my parents die."

"And this is mine." Charles Meredith IV rubbed the dresser.

They both stared at me, as I remained silent, at a loss for words.

Everyone in the room gazed at each other and put on a half smile.

I motioned to my wife that it was time to go. I never encountered such thinking with children before, and it struck me as weird. I don't ever remembering my family discussing what we were going to inherit before my parents died, not at four or five years old.

They were extremely bright children, although a little strange. Anne, in her teens, worked for me in the newsroom during the summer months and later became a screenwriter. Anne wrote the successful screenplay to *Bastard Out of Carolina*, written by Dorothy Allison. Anne moved to Los Angeles and travels with the Hollywood crowd.

Charles IV became a University of Pennsylvania graduate and attempted to run the newspaper ad department, but drifted to other jobs, doing well at them.

In 1971, his mother Ella lived above the newspaper offices after giving up her home to Charles. She had control of the money and earned a reputation of being a feisty woman whom I learned to respect. She helped proofread. A better than average drinker, after a few martinis, she could get loud and boisterous.

"I'm leaving the editorial department up to you. Write the editorials, and if something controversial comes up, we can both sit down and discuss it," Charles said.

"That's fine with me," I said.

I explained to him that I would still keep my apartment and my family in Dobbs Ferry until I found a home.

He nodded. "You'll have eight editorial employees, AP services, and features," he said. "You'll meet them when you start work."

"Thanks again, Charles." I stepped off the big porch and into my car with my family.

We stopped at Trainer's, a locally famous restaurant that was on Route 309, for dinner. We were all starving. We ordered hot roast beef sandwiches with German potato salad.

I drove away from the small borough back to New York pondering about how I would be able to adjust to this 10,000-resident community. *Oh, well it's only an hour from Philadelphia and one hour and thirty minutes from New York City. After all, there are 20 million people around us.*

Tapping the steering wheel and gazing out the window, I drove. A dead silence fell over us, like we were in a soundproof sanctuary.

Then, from out of the backseat, my daughter Carla made a humorous comment. "Daddy, where are all the people?"

"They're here, sweetheart, they're here."

Chapter 34
A Small-Town Editor Deals
with Goers and Stayers

Lasting change does not happen overnight.
Lasting change happens in infinitesimal increments:
a day, an hour, a minute, a heartbeat at a time.
—Sarah Ban Breathnach

The chilly September morning mirrored the cool reception I received from the news staff at the *Free Press*. No one came rushing up to welcome me as the new savior of this troubled small newspaper. On my first day, I called a quick meeting in the tiny newsroom to introduce myself and my plans for the paper.

"I would appreciate everyone coming in and taking a seat," I called, pointing to the front of my desk.

Charles Meredith, the publisher, who should have introduced me, was home sleeping that early fall morning in 1971. I explained to this half-asleep staff about my qualifications and what I expected.

"I want to make this the best, most aggressive small newspaper in the area. I need your help, and I am counting on you." The less-than-enthusiastic reporters gazed stone-faced at me and continued to sip on coffee and munch donuts.

"If I don't get what I need, I'll make some changes," I said. "I didn't come here from New York to be part of a failing newspaper." I attempted to give them a friendly look despite their attitude. "Any questions you have, I can answer after the meeting. I know you want the same thing as I do: first-rate reporting and a winning newspaper."

I waited a moment. No questions were asked. After the meeting, the atmosphere grew even cooler, but they got the message. I readily saw it would be almost impossible to inspire the snail-paced news staff.

Some of these reporters couldn't last five minutes on a city paper. *With a little patience, I can help them,* I thought; *if not, replace them.*

A few turned friendly after a bit. Charles kept George Fox, the previous editor, on the payroll as a sports writer. He wrote everything in longhand. Infuriated at first, I learned to live with it. I felt sorry for George, a loyal employee for thirty years, who would retire with a minimal pension if any.

Charles told me that if he couldn't learn to type and understand the new computer system, fire him. I didn't have the heart to let the guy go. He remained as a sports writer and a production paste-up man.

What the hell! Thomas Jefferson couldn't type.

The rest of the staff was green, almost amateurish. Gary Andrews, one of the reporters with a little experience, showed slight makings of a reporter, but talked more than he wrote. He bounced back and forth between sports and news.

My first call on the job was a signal of things to come.

"Can't you get anything right in that local rag?" The voice complained about his daughter's name being misspelled in her wedding picture. I learned that a country editor hears all complaints, no matter how small. It kept me busy, but I didn't mind.

Every morning, reporters would clip local stories out of the Allentown or Philadelphia newspapers and rewrite them. At first I wondered if they pirated them, committing plagiarism common in many newspapers. I had the reporters double-check clipped stories by phone and, if necessary, at the scene. It corrected some problems, but not all.

I also wanted the *Free Press* to be an independent voice to help its questionable credibility.

"I would appreciate writing the editorials as fair as possible and not with a political slant," I explained to Charles.

Charles knew it would be better for the newspaper and agreed.

Against his wishes, I joined no clubs and patronized few social events. Staying apart from the organizations helped me to make unbiased decisions and go after everyone without apologizing. I had a policy of never endorsing a candidate. It had neutralized the newspaper. With these ingredients in order, I moved to regain the newspaper's lost integrity.

The *Free Press*, like most small newspapers, provided a training ground and boot camp for reporters. Few stayed more than a year. The paper became a revolving door for young reporters, providing me often with new faces in the newsroom. There were plenty of candidates out there.

Every time you ran an ad for a reporter, you got hundreds of resumes. We started most journalism graduates at about one hundred and twenty dollars a week. Those from the Columbia School of Journalism we offered one hundred and twenty five dollars.

I did hire a few reporters who I thought could make it with a large newspaper. Ann Gerhart was one of them. She came from a Lancaster, Pennsylvania, newspaper. Her husband had a business in the area and the couple moved into central Bucks.

The writing test I gave to most applicants was not hard, but difficult to attain a hundred. Ann, an attractive, blonde-haired whiz, scored a near perfect mark. She also did everything an editor wanted from a reporter. Ann worked well alone, was accurate, and full of energy.

She worked a lot of hours and rightfully wanted to be paid for them. We did not pay overtime because the newspaper felt reporters were paid a salary to do the job and weren't entitled to receive overtime. The personnel were given time off instead, which put the newspaper into a legal bind.

We were wrong and we got hit for $16,000 worth of back pay. Ann was one who received retroactive overtime pay. I had a suspicion that she secretly notified the Department of Labor and sparked the investigation into the overtime dispute. I always thought the staff should be paid for overtime and was elated about the decision.

Ann proved to be a solid reporter and she eventually went to work for the *Philadelphia Daily News* and then the *Washington Post.* I saw her on C-Span once. I was delighted to see what she had accomplished.

Ann Gerhart ranked high on the list of good reporters, but in my opinion, Barbara Reboratti turned out to be the most superior writers and investigative reporters I hired. A former nurse, she had an eagle-eye for a good story. With extensive medical knowledge, she knew how to dig deep, and always came up with interesting stories.

One of her exciting stories was about a serial rapist who was never apprehended. The story drew wide attention and readership. And like any aggressive newspaper, we rode the story for all it was worth.

According to police, the rapist knew the area well. He mapped out isolated homes and assaulted the women living in them. With a small motorbike, he approached the house, cut the telephone lines and knocked on the door. At gunpoint, he took the husband and the children, then shoved them in the trunk of the car. After that, he raped the victim. The rapist terrorized upper Bucks for several weeks.

Barbara worked day and night on the story, and came up with solid leads. The rapist was never caught. Today he may be a man in his middle fifties.

Barbara could have worked at any newspaper, but stayed at the *Free Press* for years. She suffered a devastating personal tragedy when a drunk driver killed her daughter. It took long time for Barbara to regain her composure and then write about the tragedy.

After a few years of working long hours seven days a week, the effort paid off. The newspaper took on a slight resemblance to a decent daily newspaper. With an aggressive advertising team led by Hedl Roulette, the newspaper produced revenue that allowed for a few more reporters.

This might not be a lasting change. The worst was yet to come.

Chapter 35
Empty Tables

Seeing Florence Rizzo at the Casa D'Roma felt like a welcome breath of fresh air. She was with the news staff on Friday night unwinding over a couple of drinks. I hardly knew them anymore. I noticed the longer I spent away from the staff, the farther we seemed to drift apart. We had little in common now, and it showed it in our idle chatter.

"Are we ever going to see you again?" Florence said with a serious look on her tired face.

"Absolutely," I said, "I going to come home on the weekends for a long time, so you're not going to get rid of me that easy. And I will only be working an hour and a half away. I'll never be from far New York."

"Good," she said.

As I looked closer, I noticed how pale and worn out she appeared.

"Have you been working too hard?" I said.

"No, just tired," she said in an almost exhausted tone. "I don't know what has come over me lately. I'm sleeping more than usual."

"Have you been to a doctor?" I inquired.

"No, I'll be okay," she said.

"And how's married life?"

She just looked away and didn't answer. I didn't take it any further. I saw trouble all over her sallow face.

"How's work?"

"Same everyday shit," she answered.

I noticed David Wallace missing from the crowd. There must have been a breakup, but I decided not to pump her for any information. I felt a sense of sadness for her. I was sure things were coming apart in her life and she wanted to bury them deep inside.

"I will be in New York on the weekends and maybe we could get together for a drink, when you're feeling better," I said.

"Yeah, call me," she said. "I'm not going anywhere."

The invitation didn't seem sincere. I understood.

"Well, it's about that time," she said. "I gotta run, take care," she said as she kissed me softly on the cheek

"Someday," she said. "Someday we'll talk about it."

"You take care of yourself, Flo," I said as I watched her disappear out the door.

A strange feeling came over me. I wondered if I would ever see her again.

I downed the rest of the gin in my drink and was ready to walk out when I heard a familiar voice. It was Bill Blair.

"Don't leave, I got to talk to you," he said, his tie loose and his shirt half hanging out of his dusty trousers.

"If you buy, I'll listen," I said.

"Phil, two giant martinis," he said. "And two large black olives."

"Okay, before I get drunk from this king-size glass of gin, what's up?" I said.

"I'm leaving *Yonkers*," he said.

"I not surprised," I said. "I think you have been planning to leave for a long time."

"It's a personal matter. I'm going to try to start a new life," he said.

"My wife and I have resolved our differences and we're going to give our marriage another chance. You know, we can't have children, and we're looking into adopting," he said.

"Whoa," I said. "Don't throw too much at me at once. First, where are you going?"

"Midwest. A small newspaper in Gary, Indiana. I leave in about a month."

"If you're going to adopt, why don't you go back to the Spanish girl you got pregnant and set it up to adopt her baby," I suggested.

Bill remained silent.

"Hey, are you listening to me?" I asked.

"I heard you," he said. "I heard you."

"Well?"

"The last time I talked to you, she was going to get an abortion if I didn't marry her, right?" he said.

"I hope you talked some sense into her," I said.

"No, I didn't," he said.

"I told her I was married and I wasn't going to leave my wife for her. I told her she should have the baby and find some nice Spanish guy and settle down. There's lots of single mothers who marry. Times are changing. It's not taboo. I told her I would pay for the delivery, but she would have to take care of it," he said.

I had to hold my Italian temper. I wanted to strangle the son of bitch. *He left her alone and she would have no choice but to abort the child,* I thought. *What a jerk. What a user.*

"Go on, tell me the rest," I said.

"Well, there's not much more to tell," he said. "It's been two months and I haven't heard a word from her. Do you think she had the baby?"

"I don't know," I said. "But you gave her little choice. A stupid move on your part. You should have at least tried to help her instead of pulling the trap door on her. At twenty, she's going to do the wrong thing," I said.

"Now, you'll never know if you have a daughter or a son out there. Maybe it doesn't matter," I said. "It happens every day. If I had a nickel for every guy that knocks up a woman and dumps her, I would be a billionaire."

I waited a bit and continued. "I told you the last time we talked that you could have talked her into having the baby and then adopted it if she didn't want it."

"Well, I got chicken-shit and panicked," Bill said.

"Do you think I will even see her again? When are you leaving for

Gary, Indiana?"

"I told you before, about a month," he said.

"My answer is no, you'll never see her again. That's my bet," I said.

"Never is a long time," Bill said.

"Well, maybe someday. You get a knock on the door and when you open it you may find your son of daughter there. Then you'll hear, 'Are you the asshole father who dumped me twenty years ago?'"

"Stop the shit," Bill said. "I feel terrible."

He added, "Maybe she had an abortion, and my worries are over."

"Are they?" I asked, then abruptly cut the conversation.

"I'm starting to get drunk. I better head for home."

"Are we going to get together before I leave?" Bill asked.

"Sure," I said. "Call me next week."

"Don't let me go without saying goodbye," he said.

"Never," I said as I eased my way into my car and pulled away. I never saw or heard of Bill again.

I saw little of Florence and Jill after moving to Pennsylvania. Both wanted to let go of the past and stay on a fresh career course. We all did.

I received one letter from Florence suggesting lunch if I ever got to New York again. I thought someday, but we all needed a new life and a departure from the outrageous '60s.

After being promoted to General Manger of a Gannett newspaper in North Tarrytown, New York, Florence fell seriously ill. She died in a New York City hospital, with her sister at her bedside.

Jill, who became a tough *Yonkers* editor, died a few years later. Both died of cancer. I never knew Florence was dying and learned about her death months later from a trade magazine. No doubt, I would have quickly visited her if I knew she was ill. Ironically, the bad news never reached me. Those around her thought I was unimportant. Perhaps it was too painful for her to see me and relive the past at a terrible state in her life.

She was a dear friend and a wonderful human being.

The rest of the *Yonkers* editorial staff scattered. Bob Martin would be fired and disappeared in the Midwest. David Wallace was promoted in the chain. Barney Waters would head south again and work for *USA Today*. I saw Barney years later in Cocoa Beach. We had a drink, engaged in some small talk. He told me about Martin Greco, my old boss at the *Orlando Sentinel*. Greco left the *Sentinel* and started his own weekly. I saw Marty for a few minutes. He was wearing a white mask and coping with cancer. We parted quickly; we had little to say to one another.

Time to move on and take my family and the memories with me.

Time to leave the empty tables in the Casa D'Roma and focus on a new life.

Chapter 36
The Streaking Publisher

There is nothing more frightful than ignorance in action.

—Johann von Goethe

Working for a family-owned newspaper has it quirks, but nothing was so bizarre as working for Charles Meredith III.

"Hey, how about Charles Meredith and one of his friends streaking around town on a cold winter night," a salesperson said. I had heard he and some friends were joking around and he ran streaking around his house. I never found out what the story really was. An employee doesn't bring something like this up to his boss.

We seldom socialized and our relationship consisted of business only. At the few seminars we attended together, even newspaper functions, we stayed apart. Charles stood close to his mother and wife. He mingled with a few publishers, smoked long black cigarettes, and drank white wine. I knew little about his family and he had practically no knowledge of or interest in mine.

Charles did surprise me one morning in his office. When his daughter became a teenager, she worked in the newsroom during the summer months as an obituary writer and did a fine job. Anne was the quietest reporter in the newsroom, almost too quiet. She never spoke to her father while working, not even a good morning.

That morning, he shut the door to his office. "Did you see that my daughter has holes in her jeans?"

"I didn't notice," I replied.

"Well, you better tell her to get them fixed."

"Charles, she's your daughter, you tell her." He didn't answer. She lived in his home and it was his responsibility to talk to her about her jeans at home.

I walked out and saw Anne's jeans, but said nothing to her. Today it's normal for teens to walk around with a hole in jeans, fashionable, even. In the '70s, it was strange.

The Meredith family were not popular employers. The rich are often looked upon with contempt, often unfairly. Maybe it was jealousy. The Merediths were cheap employers. The employees were unbelievably underpaid. Once a year, management might break down and give an employee a ten-cent raise.

When I arrived, the *Free Press* had no pension plan for its workers. Later, Woody Lewis, a forty-year production employee, retired with a one-hundred-dollar-a-month pension. Most retired with no pension or health insurance. At that sorry time, I was part of the management team and had to painfully find a way to support the unpleasant working conditions.

Now and then the workers got restless and smoldered about the low wages. In 1972, with the employees ready to explode and stage a walkout, Charles called an emergency management meeting and with much anxiety explained about the rebellion that could take place.

"I have heard that the pressroom and production workers are going to strike for better conditions," he told us.

"I don't blame them," whispered one of the ad directors.

Charles seemed in a state of shock. He looked pale; there were sweat beads on his forehead.

"After all the good my father and this newspaper did for our workers, this is the thanks we get."

I wasn't aware that the Meredith family had done much for them. This threatened strike was the backlash of not taking care of good employees.

"Well, if they do strike, we'll have to roll up our sleeves and get this newspaper out," he said.

We looked at each other and giggled. I think most of the people in the room were pulling for the workers.

As it turned out, they did not strike. Most couldn't afford to be out of work a day. Charles emerged the victor.

The *Free Press* had a plantation mentality. A master-servant relationship prevailed.

The Christmas parties were meager. The Yule gathering was held in the pressroom with roast beef sandwiches and potato chips served. A piano was rolled in. Charles played the piano and the employees sang Christmas carols. There were no Christmas bonuses, nothing but the tinny sound of the piano to bring in the holiday. I never attended the so-called festivities.

All companies have spies and ass kissers. The *Free Press* was no different. Bookkeeper Josephine Stover stayed very closed to Charles's father. She was Charles' eyes and ears, always keeping close tabs on all employees, even listening to their telephone calls. A wealthy widow, Josephine worked for fifty years for the newspaper.

Charles had a touch of paranoia in him. Although he talked about the "family" workers, inside his soul, he knew he wasn't the best-liked man in the newspaper. He always thought the workers were talking about him.

I remember one day outside my office, I was talking with Art Morak, one of the ad directors, when Charles walked out on his way home. He left the office and returned through the back door, apparently to press his ear to his office door and listen to those of us outside it. When he came out from the closed door, we both laughed.

"I forgot my book," he said. A look of embarrassment came over his face.

A small community has the same problems that a large city has: murders, political corruption, and crime. Upper Bucks was no different. I attempted to cover those stories with as much fact-finding as the little staff could bear. We struck hard, despite Charles' grumbling, at government secrecy such as closed school board and township meetings.

I wrote dozens of editorials pushing to open secret meetings in the area, and as a result, the newspaper nominated me for a Pulitzer Prize for editorial writing in 1977. I did not win, but it gave me a good feeling about my integrity as an editor.

Although the *Free Press* won dozens of awards when I was editor, I put little stock in them. It may have displayed a little of the talent to our peers, but in my opinion, journalism prizes really mean very little.

Even with the weird publisher, the showboating prizes gave the *Free Press* a smidgen of intellectual muscle. The awards also resulted in giving the newspaper the strongest voice the paper had enjoyed since the first publisher, Charles I, and the sheriff participated in hanging a thief in the county a hundred years before.

Chapter 37
The Confederate
Captain-Turned-Ad Director

Perhaps even these things, one day,
will be pleasing to remember.
— Virgil, *Aeneid*

Art Morak, Advertising Director for the *Free Press*, smoked king-sized cigarettes, slicked his light brown hair straight back, and flashed steel gray eyes. Art, a slim, well-spoken and polite thirty-year-old, did have some strange ways about him.

A staunch believer in looking to the stars for guidance, he explained to anyone who would listen that this was his second time walking on earth. In his previous life, he died in a Civil War battle.

Art and I became good friends. Our chemistry and views on sports and world events were the same until he started to talk about the stars and living another life.

"I was killed on the battlefield near Gettysburg. I often visit the spot where I fell," he told me.

I blinked my eyes. "What?"

He repeated what he had said.

"You've got to be kidding me, right?

"No, I'm dead serious. I was a captain in the Confederate Army," he said.

"Why did you come back as an ad director?" I asked. "To drive the publisher nuttier than he already is?"

"This isn't the end of the road for me," he said.

"If you say so." I shrugged my shoulders.

I think he was a little shy to go any further. We let it go at that.

Art possessed immense charm with women, almost hypnotic. His piercing gray eyes and diamond-shaped face mesmerized females. June Marley*, a married reporter, was attracted to him at first sight.

The minute they met, she connected. She loved his philosophy and his view of the cosmos. The couple spent hours talking about the stars, the afterlife, and the signals coming out of the heavens.

"Don't you find him bright and intriguing?" June said to anyone who would listen.

The newsroom buzzed about their open relationship. At lunch the lovebirds walked down Quakertown's sidewalks, holding hands, laughing, looking in the store windows, and enjoying the lovely summer days. It had signs of a passionate love affair; but it was simply a combination of compatible minds. I don't think Art ever went to bed with June. He wanted to be with her especially during the daytime. It was the strangest relationship I ever witnessed.

Charles never spoke to me about it, but his mother, annoyed by it all, called me into her office and wanted an explanation.

"Have you seen June and Art parading around town, holding hands?" the sixty-five-year-old assistant publisher asked.

"I can't control people when they're not at work," I said. "As long as the two are not embarrassing the newspaper, I can't interfere. Right now, it's none of my concern." I didn't know what else to say.

I don't think she liked the answer, but that was the end of it as far as I was concerned.

Art's dislike for Charles spilled over to the sales staff. They thought the publisher was a clown. Art saw Charles as a spoiled, rich brat who had everything handed to him except newspaper integrity. For Charles, the feeling was mutual. He wanted more revenue from the sales department and thought Art was lazy. Charles resented Art's talking almost openly about what he perceived to be mismanagement. The stormy feud headed for a showdown.

A few months later, in the fall of 1975, Charles, tormented by Art's attitude, fired him. Later in the day, Charles called me into his office and explained why he fired the star-gazing ad director.

"Art did not produce the business we needed, and he has been saying some pretty nasty things about our family."

"It's your newspaper," I said and walked out of his office. The issue never surfaced again.

I walked over to Art's office. "Sorry to see you leave, fellow, but a man with your talent won't be out of work long." I knew he wanted to leave anyway.

"I feel relieved that I'm out of here. In fact, I knew it was going to happen." Art put his hand on my shoulder. "I enjoyed working with you. It's nice to work with a real newspaper editor."

"Thanks, and let's keep in touch," I said.

"Sure," he said. I watched while he cleaned out his desk and then walked out the door. I smiled.

"I don't know if I should salute you or shake your hand, Captain," I said.

We both laughed and hugged.

I watched him walk out the narrow hallway to the front door and felt a little empty. I knew I would miss his company.

I heard he went to work for a newspaper outside of Philadelphia, and then I lost track of him. I never saw him or heard from him again. June resigned a few months later and got a big public relations job in New Jersey. She called me once and I wasn't home. I would have liked to talk with her. Maybe another time.

Or another lifetime.

Chapter 38
The Final Days
at the *Free Press*

If Charles Meredith III was the publisher of the *Washington Post* at the time of Watergate, chances are he would have fired the two reporters, Bob Woodward and Carl Bernstein, along with the editor, Ben Bradley. President Richard Nixon would have completed his term as President and the United States would have avoided the biggest political scandal in American history. We would have failed to test the Constitution that proves the President of the United States is not above the law.

Unlike the gutsy *Washington Post* Publisher, Katherine Graham, Meredith panicked when he saw the words *sources said* or *it has been reported* or that an action was *questioned*. Newspapers sometimes need these tools to protect unidentified sources and move government agencies to reveal information that many times would be kept secret.

Investigative reporting terrified Meredith. He was paranoid to the degree that he did not trust his editors or reporters. I found out while working for him that he had trouble believing that elected officials should be held to the highest standards in the land. He couldn't understand that newspapers acted as watchdogs over the government and that if politicians blinked, the press had not only an obligation, but also a responsibility to report it. Like some other publishers in the country, he would rather sink the potential powerhouse story than question the action of a politician. Being a politician himself made him leery of the press, the very institution that for three generations had made the Merediths wealthy. It was my belief that Charles, as did a few other publishers, thought those news stories were made to wrap around ads.

Meredith's scary publishing expertise surfaced in late 1979 when the *Free Press's* Carl Davies, an excellent investigative reporter, wrote a series revealing that Bucks County Judge William Rufe owned property in Bucks County and he was trying to develop townhouses. In the series, he stated that Judge Rufe sought help from Herb Barness, a millionaire contractor and one of the most powerful Republicans in the state of Pennsylvania, as well as being a close friend of President Nixon's. Barness's gigantic construction company was always in front of the Bucks County Courts, seeking an array of legal rulings. Keeping company with Barness presented a potentially conflicting position for Judge Rufe.

Any newspaper with even minuscule credentials would have jumped on the story. When a judge is trying to develop land in his jurisdiction and seeks the help of a powerful king maker, that is news. A judge must stand the toughest scrutiny of all elected officials. His activity must always stay in the public eye.

The *Free Press* ran a series of articles, which were researched thoroughly, with no unnamed sources in the articles. We double-checked all the facts. County documents were used to support the story. Calls to the judge were not returned. The fact that the judge never commented on a story, I thought, showed that it was accurate.

The newspaper received no complaints about the series. Not one reader questioned the story, and in fact, the newspaper was praised for its coverage. Everyone was satisfied except one person: Publisher Charles Meredith III.

"The story made the judge look like a bad person," he said later. "I didn't like the tone of the story."

Meredith admitted that no one had approached him to say that the stories were slanted against the judge or inaccurate.

The day after the final series ran in the newspaper, Charles called me in his office.

I saw the front page of the newspaper on his desk with "Apology" written across the story about Judge Rufe dealing with land development.

"This kind of story cannot run in this newspaper," he said in a near fit. His hand shook and his lips quivered.

"What's wrong with the story?" I asked.

"I don't the like words, *Judge Questioned* in the headline. It's like the newspaper is questioning the judge's integrity."

"When a judge's business relationship with a contractor who comes before the court almost weekly for zoning changes and other problems, we have a right to ask whether the relationship is a little sensitive and may lead to a conflict of interest," I said. "Keep in mind that this judge wanted to develop this property in his jurisdiction," I added.

"Charles, the story was absolutely correct and we have used no unnamed sources. Much of the information was taken from public records. I don't know what the problem is," I continued. "We can't cover up a judge's mistakes, *especially* a judge," I continued.

Still adamant about the story, he shouted, "I don't want this to happen again in this newspaper!"

I didn't say a word. I just gazed at this confused human being. *Did he want me to apologize for writing the truth?*

"I want you to fire Davies," he said.

I was stunned. I couldn't believe what I was hearing. He wanted to fire a reporter who had done nothing wrong, and in fact, deserved credit for digging hard and writing the story. I knew it wasn't his kind of story, but as an editor, I knew it had to be written.

I looked at him and thought about my own integrity as an editor and what I thought might seem like a coverup if we backed down on the story. And, to make it even worse, he wanted me to write a front-page apology for a story that had no errors in it. Charles wanted me to prostitute my editorial experience, everything I believed in, to satisfy his unfounded fears.

I thought of the long, hard years I had worked to prepare the newspaper for some credibility, the many arguments with the publisher about good story ideas. I thought of the long hours I had dedicated to make the *Free Press* a reputable newspaper. I thought about my family coming to Pennsylvania and my daughters going to fine schools. *Should I throw all that away for a story?*

I knew Charles would not change his mind. If there was something wrong with the judge's involvement in the development project, I did not want to become part of a coverup. Whatever the outcome, I had my own dignity as a journalist to protect.

There were more questions buzzing around in my mind. *Was I willing to keep the comfortable security I had and go out and fire the reporter and remain on staff like a journalistic traitor? On the other hand, did I want to throw away everything I had worked for nine years over a story that readers would forget in a couple of days?*

I faced the most critical decision I had to make since I left Olean to start an uncharted newspaper career. How much are integrity and honesty worth? I know that many decisions are made at newspapers that are not always in the best interest of the public. They are made because of personal interest. This case of "freedom of the press" was for the one who *owned* the press. *Who the hell was I to play martyr and destroy my career?*

No one really cared. Most readers believed the press was loaded with errors and mistakes anyway. One more wouldn't make a difference. Few Americans see heroes in the press. Many intensely dislike the press.

For a second, I thought: *Fire Davies and go back and go through the moves of an editor, get paid, and live happily after.* I knew that whatever decision I made, my family and I were going to pay dearly. *What was the right decision?*

I was an insignificant part of the scenario. As my Park Bench Gang buddies might have described it, I was a pisshole in the snow. What I did would have no impact on the business. This wasn't the movies where there was a happy ending. The only ones who would suffer would be the ones I loved the most. Since Charles was a member of the prestigious American Publishers Association, the best I could get was fired and blackballed.

I remembered what my first editor, Wilson McGee, told me in my first interview working for the *Orlando Sentinel.* "Get the facts rights and stick by them. That's what you are here for and that's newspapers are all about. Tell the truth." Anything else would be whoredom.

I stood up in the office chair and looked down on this little publisher who now owned a newspaper worth five million dollars. What I had to say in the next minutes would change my life forever.

"If you want to fire him, do it yourself," I said. "I won't sweep the truth under a rug."

He looked at me almost with glee, as if he had expected my reaction.

I walked out of his office.

A few minutes later, he wrote a one-sentence letter firing me, which was delivered by his loyal bookkeeper, Josephine Stover. She was at her best when it came to giving departed workers their last paycheck for her boss, Charles.

"Here is your final check," she said crisply. "And leave the company car here." I didn't have a ride back to my apartment and they knew it.

And, just like that, a 25-year newspaper career was on the brink of oblivion.

I called a cab, turned in my keys, and cleaned out my desk.

It was a Saturday and no one was in the building, so I didn't have a chance to say goodbye to the staff. I looked around to see if I forgot anything, then walked down the narrow hallway, out into the street, where I calmly waited for my cab.

After I closed the front door behind me, I heard a large bang, like the sound of a brass lock shutting the door tight, finalizing my time at the *Free Press.*

As the cab moved up Broad Street, we passed Liberty Hall, a place where, in 1777, the Liberty Bell had been hidden the from the British Army. I asked the cab driver to slow down for a moment.

I looked intensely at the small stone house and for a moment, I thought about the group of revolutionaries driving a wagon with the Liberty Bell on it alongside the building. The bell, which chimed on

July 8, 1776 for the first reading of the Declaration of Independence, would have been a few feet from where I was. The bell had made a historic journey from England to Philadelphia, and then to Quakertown, and finally was hidden in Allentown. Farmers and revolutionary men risked their lives over this cracked Liberty Bell, which became a symbol of freedom. Although the bell was mere metal, if it had been left behind in Philadelphia, it might have been swallowed into the sands of history and forgotten. However, a handful of freedom fighters decided not to abandon this symbol of freedom.

I had passed Liberty Hall a thousand times during my eight years in Quakertown, but gazing at it from the slow-moving cab, I saw it in a much brighter light. Overwhelmed by the glow and the symbolism, I felt a sense of pride, and a sense of resolve I shall never forget.

With a sigh of relief, I felt at peace with what I had done. The decision not to change the truth was worth the difficulty the future would bring. By not doing what I believed was right, there would no future for me.

"Did you see enough?" said the impatient cab driver, tapping his fingers on the steering wheel.

I closed my eyes and fell into a serene state of mind.

"We can go now."

The cab sped away and my search for a new life took hold again. In a few weeks, I had other job offers and new possibilities.

Epilogue

The daily *Free Press* would eventually become a weekly. The *Herald Statesman* closed. The *Newark News* closed. The *Mount Vernon Argus* closed. The *Hudson Dispatch* closed. Five of the eight newspapers are no longer operating.

Printed in the United States
103937LV00002B/112/A

9 781413 748819